英汉对照世界名著文库

Beauty and the Beast

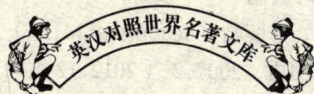

英汉对照世界名著文库

Beauty and the Beast

美女与野兽

[法] 普兰斯·德·博蒙特 著

翟自洋 译

中国书店

图书在版编目（CIP）数据

美女与野兽 /（法）博蒙特（Beaumont, M.D.）著；翟自
洋译.—北京：中国书店，2007.2（2012.12 重印）
（英汉对照世界名著文库. 第 5 辑）
ISBN 978-7-80663-209-3

Ⅰ.①美… Ⅱ.①博… ②翟… Ⅲ.①英语－汉语－
对照读物 ②童话－法国－近代 Ⅳ.①H319.4：Ⅰ

中国版本图书馆 CIP 数据核字（2011）第 030875 号

英汉对照世界名著文库（第 5 辑） 美女与野兽

作　　者：（法）博蒙特（Beaumont, M.D.）
译　　者：翟自洋
责任编辑：杨　颖
装帧设计：李艾红
美术编辑：穆　红
文字编辑：赵　晴

出版发行：**中国书店**
地　　址：北京市宣武区琉璃厂东街 115 号
邮　　编：100050
经　　销：全国新华书店
印　　刷：北京一鑫印务有限责任公司
开　　本：635mm × 940mm　1/16
版　　次：2007 年 2 月第 1 版　2012 年 12 月第 2 次印刷
字　　数：1247 千字
印　　张：108
书　　号：ISBN 978-7-80663-209-3
定　　价：238.40 元（全 8 册）

出版说明

为给广大英语爱好者提供一套便捷、有效地学习英语的理想读本，我们编辑出版了这套《英汉对照世界名著文库》系列丛书。其中收录了世界文学史上影响最大、价值最高、流传最广的经典名著，采用英汉对照的方式，旨在帮助广大英语爱好者通过读名著来学习英文。该丛书具有以下四个特点：

一、权威主编　质量一流

本丛书由著名翻译家宋兆霖先生担任主编，所选经典名著无论英文还是译文，都具有很高的文学艺术价值。我们试图通过这一努力，改变国内英汉对照名著良莠杂陈、令读者无所适从的现状。

二、一书两用　物超所值

名著是人类智慧的结晶，文辞优美，结构严谨，具有巨大的思想和艺术魅力。本丛书采用左英右汉的对照形式，帮助读者对照学习。使读者既可以阅读世界名著、陶冶情操、提高修养，又可以培养学习兴趣、提高英语读写能力，双重收获，效率倍增。

三、原汁英语　经典名著

本丛书除收录部分英、美等国作家的原著，对于非英语语言的名著，则由国内外知名的英语专家、学者以精准、流畅的英语重新编写，既保留了原著的精华，又使作品变得浅显易懂，从而避免了长篇名著的晦涩难懂。结合通俗、生动的译文，使读者能够准确地把握名著的精髓。

四、精编精释　理想读本

本丛书依照词汇量的多少及语法结构的难易程度，分为易、中、难三大部分，不同的读者既可以按不同的需求选择阅读，也可以由易到难，系统地学习。结合译作者精当的注释，以及相应的词汇表，帮助读者扫除阅读中的障碍，全面、深入、高效地阅读世界名著。

ABOUT THE AUTHOR

Jeanne-Marie le Prince was born in Rouen, France, in 1711. In 1743, she married a man named Beaumont. The marriage lasted only two years, but she kept her husband's last name.

In 1746, Beaumont moved to England. There she wrote novels and short stories based on her work as a governess and tutor. In 1748, her first novel was published in France.

In 1756, she wrote her own version of *Beauty and the Beast.* The original story by Madame Gabrielle de Villaneuve had been written for adults. Beaumont's version was aimed at a younger audience.

Beaumont wrote more than seventy books, fairy tales, and short stories. Her emphasis on selfless love and happy endings has influenced fairy tale literature for more than three centuries. She died in 1780.

关 于 作 者

珍妮·玛丽·普兰斯 1711 年生于法国鲁昂。1743 年，她嫁给一个名叫博蒙特的人。这段婚姻只维持了两年时间，可是她一直保留着夫姓。

1746 年，博蒙特搬到伦敦。她在那儿以自己家庭教师的工作为素材，创作长短篇小说。1748 年，她的第一部小说在法国出版。

1756 年，她开始创作自己的《美女与野兽》。这个故事原本是加布里埃尔·德·维兰努夫人为成人而作的，博蒙特的版本则是针对青少年读者。

博蒙特写了 70 多部书，主要是童话故事和短篇小说。她强调无私的爱，作品结局多美满快乐，3 个世纪以来她的创作一直影响着童话文学。她于 1780 年去世。

CONTENTS

Prologue 12

1. Beauty 14

2. The Merchant 18

3. Beauty's Sisters 22

4. A Letter Brings New Hope 26

5. More Disappointments 30

6. Lost in the Woods 36

7. The Great Castle 40

8. The Next Morning 46

9. The Beast 50

10. Treasures from the Castle 58

11. A Bittersweet Reunion 62

目 录

序 言 13

一、贝 蒂 15

二、商 人 19

三、贝蒂的姐姐 23

四、一封带来新希望的信 27

五、更大的失望 31

六、在森林里迷路 37

七、宏伟的城堡 41

八、第二天早上 47

九、野 兽 51

十、城堡里的财宝 59

十一、悲喜交集的团圆 63

12. Beauty's Decision 68

13. Beauty Goes to the Beast's Castle 74

14. A Sad Farewell 82

15. Beauty's Room 90

16. Visions 96

17. An Evening Together 102

18. The First Proposal 108

19. Encore 112

20. Time Passes 118

21. Shadows in the Moonlight 122

22. The Magical Theater 126

23. Beauty's Request.. 132

24. A Family Reunion 136

25. Envy Everlasting 146

26. The Dream 150

27. Searching for the Beast 154

28. No Longer a Beast 160

十二、贝蒂的决定 69

十三、贝蒂前往野兽的城堡 75

十四、伤感的离别 83

十五、贝蒂的房间 91

十六、幻　影 97

十七、晚上的碰面 103

十八、第一次求婚 109

十九、再次求婚 113

二十、时光流逝 119

二十一、月光下的阴影 123

二十二、神奇的剧场 127

二十三、贝蒂的请求 133

二十四、合家团圆 137

二十五、无休止的嫉妒 147

二十六、梦　境 151

二十七、寻找野兽 155

二十八、野兽变身 161

29. The Evil Fairy 166

30. Reliving the Past 170

31. A Wedding at the Great Hall 178

Epilogue 184

二十九、邪恶的精灵 167

三十、往日再现 171

三十一、大厅里的婚礼 179

尾　声 185

词汇表 186

PROLOGUE

Deep in the woods, where fairies and sprites, imps and ogres still exert power over mortals, stands a castle. Unseen by passersby, the lonely castle remains silent except for the pitiful sighs of its forlorn master.

He no longer knows how long he has walked through the empty halls and grounds of his isolated estate. As time passes, he wanders alone and waits ... and waits ... and waits ...

序　言

　　森林的深处有一座城堡，在那里，各路精灵、妖魔、鬼怪依然用魔法控制着人类。没有哪个路人能看到这城堡。它孤独地静静地矗立在那里，只传来绝望的城堡主人那令人同情的叹息。

　　在空荡荡的大厅里、在孤零零的领地上，他不知徘徊了多久。时间不断流逝，他独自徘徊着、守候着……守候着……继续守候着……

1

BEAUTY

Beauty woke at dawn, as was her custom since coming to live in the country. Usually the first rays of the sun entering the small circular window of her room in the loft of the cottage woke her from her dreams. But today, it was the onset of winter's chill and the sound of her brothers yelling.

"Beauty, where is our breakfast?" Claude asked.

"We must get an early start today," Henri called up the stairs of the country home where the family had come to live this past year.

For a moment longer. Beauty lingered beneath the covers. In her dream, she and her family were well dressed and enjoying an *elegant*[1] evening in town. *Handsome* suitors were competing for her sisters' attention. The youngest of the children, she was on her father's arm as they left the concert hall with her brothers trailing behind.

---

1. 本书正文中的斜体英文在文末词汇表中均有注释。——编者注

一

贝 蒂

自从搬到乡下，贝蒂总是习惯性地在天刚亮的时候醒来。她家农舍阁楼上有扇小小的圆窗，通常清晨第一缕曙光从这里照进来，把她从睡梦中唤醒。不过今天，她是被冬日的严寒，还有哥哥们的叫喊声惊醒的。

"贝蒂，我们的早饭呢？"克劳德问。
"今天我们得早点开始。"亨利朝楼梯上大叫。贝蒂一家是去年搬到这座乡村的房子住下的。

贝蒂在被窝里又躺了一会儿。她刚做了个梦，在梦里，她和家人穿着漂亮的衣服，在镇上度过了一个美好的夜晚。英俊的追求者竞相吸引她们姐妹的注意。离开音乐厅的时候，作为家里最小的孩子，贝蒂依偎在父亲的肩膀上，哥哥则跟在他们后头。

Beauty was only sixteen years of age. She had a good heart and a pleasant *disposition* and knew some things in life were beyond one's control. Unlike her sisters and brothers. Beauty met every day with a smile and a happy heart. What she couldn't change, she accepted and made the most of.

In fact, during the past year she had worked hard and found that both her physical strength and her character were none the worse for the experience.

Beauty had many friends and admirers, all of whom knew that her physical beauty was only a hint of the loveliness of her heart.

"I'm coming," she answered, throwing the covers aside. She dressed quickly in a modest dress and apron. Then, after tying up her hair with a ribbon, she ran down the stairs to begin her daily routine of cooking and housekeeping.

贝蒂年仅十六岁，她心地善良、乐观可亲，她知道生活中有些事情是人无法控制的。贝蒂每天都是面带笑容、心情愉快，不像她的哥哥姐姐们成日里愁眉苦脸。对那些她没法改变的事情，贝蒂安于接收并且尽量让它们变得对自己有利。

事实上，在过去的一年里，她干起活来不辞辛劳，她发现自己的体力和性情并没有因为辛苦劳作而变糟。

贝蒂有许多朋友和仰慕者，他们心里都清楚，贝蒂漂亮的外形只是她美丽心灵的折射。

"我来啦。"贝蒂掀开被子，回应哥哥。她迅速穿上朴素的衣服，戴上围裙，用带子把头发扎起来，然后跑下楼，开始她每天的工作——做饭和处理家务。

2

THE MERCHANT

"Good morning, Father," Beauty said, hugging him. While his sons took their seats at the table, he looked up from the morning letters, smiled, and returned a warm hug acknowledging his favorite daughter's presence.

When Beauty's father had learned that his fortune was lost as a result of bad luck and *dishonest* clerks, he had moved his family from their town house to their country home more than one hundred miles away.

It upset his children greatly since they had to give up the lavish way of life that their father's wealth had afforded them. They had become accustomed to the very best that money could buy. Now that they were poor. Beauty and her siblings had to work the land and manage *livestock* for a living.

Beauty worked hard every day while her proud sisters grumbled and refused to lift a finger to help. Elise and Rene were very put out by the mere thought of having to work and

二

商　人

"早上好，父亲。"贝蒂拥抱父亲，向他问候。当两个儿子到餐桌旁坐下时，贝蒂的父亲在读早上收到的信件。这时，他抬起头，面带微笑，热情地拥抱贝蒂，向心爱的女儿表示感谢。

由于时运不佳，兼之手下职员欺诈，贝蒂的父亲倾家荡产了。他得知消息后，只好把家从镇上的大宅搬到一百多英里外的乡下农舍里。

从前父亲家产丰厚的时候，孩子们过着奢侈的生活。现在，他们不得不放弃这种生活，这让他们心烦意乱。以前他们过惯了锦衣玉食的生活，现在他们变得一贫如洗，贝蒂和她的哥哥姐姐不得不到地里干活、喂养牲口，以维持生计。

贝蒂每天不辞辛劳地干活，可是，她那两个高傲的姐姐却成天牢骚满腹，不肯出一点儿力帮帮她。一想到她们不得不住在乡下，还要亲自干活，伊莉斯和雷内就感到恼怒万

live in the country. They taunted their little sister for having so cheerfully accepted what could not be changed.

"Look at our little Beauty," Elise would tease, "happy to be sweeping."

"Beauty, when you finish that chore, run and fetch my pillow," Rene demanded whenever Beauty had her hands full with dishes or *laundry*.

Beauty never complained about her sisters' mean behavior toward her, although she was often made to suffer by their cruel actions.

The decline in the family's status made Beauty's brothers sad, too, but they grudgingly accepted their lot. Like their father, they were grateful for such a good-hearted sister.

The merchant knew that each of his children met the challenges that life brought them differently. He was grateful for Beauty's high spirits and hard work, but he did his best to ease the burdens that had come on the family as a result of his misfortune.

分。她们讥笑自己的小妹妹，因为她居然如此兴高采烈地接受这个事实。

"看看我们的小贝蒂，连打扫卫生都这么开心。"伊莉斯嘲弄她。

"贝蒂，做完这些家务后，上楼去把我的枕头拿下来。"无论贝蒂是忙着洗碗碟还是洗衣服，雷内总会提出要求。

虽然姐姐经常无情地对待她，可是贝蒂从来没有抱怨姐姐的这些卑劣行为。

家道中落同样让贝蒂的两个哥哥感到悲哀，他们心有不甘，但也只得勉强接受命运的安排。他们跟父亲一样，对这个好心肠的妹妹充满了感激。

商人心里清楚，他的每个孩子都以不同的态度面对生活带给他们的挑战。他感激贝蒂总是快快乐乐、辛勤劳作，同时，他自己也竭尽所能，以减轻生意失败给家人带来的负担。

3

BEAUTY'S SISTERS

Elise and Rene were not only jealous of Beauty's lovely features, but were angry because she was kind and sincere.

Beauty's sisters were known by all to be prideful and arrogant. During the days of the family's prosperity, when they lived in town in a lovely home with servants, they often shunned the company of the daughters and wives of other prosperous merchants, businessmen, and landowners, believing themselves to be better than everyone else.

They also scorned the advances of the most prosperous suitors, preferring to wait to marry a duke or an earl at the very least. They considered anyone untitled to be beneath them.

Although Elise and Rene treated their suitors badly, when their father lost his fortune, the haughty girls were certain that they could arrange a quick match and marry well.

But those suitors disappeared when they learned that the

三

贝蒂的姐姐

伊莉斯和雷内不仅嫉妒贝蒂可爱的容貌，而且对她的善良、真诚也感到愤怒。

贝蒂那两个姐姐高傲自大，这是大家都知道的。家境富裕的时候，她们住在镇上漂亮的房子里，还有仆人伺候。那时，她们常常故意避开其他富商和地主妻女，因为她们自认为比所有人都优越。

她们还蔑视那些最有钱的追求者，她们的心愿是等着某位公爵或者至少是伯爵大人来迎娶自己。在她们看来，那些连封号都没有的家伙怎么配得上自己呢。

尽管伊莉斯和雷内对她们的追求者态度恶劣，可是当父亲破产的时候，这两个傲慢的姑娘仍然深信她们可以迅速找个好人家，风风光光地嫁人。

然而，得知她们家一贫如洗后，追求者马上就消失得无

family was now poor. None of those fine gentlemen wanted to take a penniless, proud wife.

In fact, everyone who knew them believed that the mean-spirited sisters had finally gotten what they deserved.

While the neighbors secretly enjoyed Elise and Rene's hardship, they were heartbroken that Beauty suffered. The family's friends cared about Beauty's fate since she was a most wonderful and deserving person.

Elise and Rene hated Beauty now more than ever because Beauty's many suitors still wanted to marry her.

Beauty was consoled by her suitors' concern for her future, but she felt she was too young to marry. Instead, she chose to stay with her father to help him during this difficult time.

Her suitors graciously understood her decision, wished her well, and remained her dear friends.

影无踪。那些花花公子们没有一个愿意娶身无分文却又傲慢自大的妻子。

事实上，认识她们的人都相信，生性卑劣的两姐妹终于落得了应有的下场。

左邻右舍为伊莉斯和雷内的困苦暗自高兴，与此同时，又为贝蒂的遭遇感到悲伤。她家的朋友关心贝蒂今后的命运，因为她最出色、最应该得到生活的回报。

如今，贝蒂的许多追求者依然想娶她为妻，这让伊莉斯和雷内对她更加憎恨。

追求者关心贝蒂的前途，这让她感到安慰。可是，她觉得自己还太小，不该这么早结婚。她选择留在父亲身边，帮助他渡过难关。

贝蒂的追求者体谅她的决定，祝福她一切顺利，并且继续做她的好朋友。

4

A LETTER BRINGS NEW HOPE

While Beauty was cleaning up after the morning meal, her father rose from his chair and waved a letter in the air.

"Good news has finally come!" he shouted. "One of the ships has arrived at last! I must go and see what I can get by selling the merchandise."

Wakened by the commotion, Elise and Rene came running down the steps in their nightgowns and robes.

"Oh, Father, we'll be rich again," Elise shouted.

"We can leave this dreadful house and move back to town," added Claude.

"We'll be rich gentlemen again," Henri said aloud dreamily.

"Father, bring us back new gowns and shoes and hats," demanded Rene.

26

四

一封带来新希望的信

吃过早饭，贝蒂正在打扫卫生。这时，父亲从椅子上站起来，挥舞着手里的一封信。

"好消息终于来啦！"他大叫起来，"有一艘船最终靠岸了！我得去看看卖掉船上的货物我还能赚多少钱。"

伊莉斯和雷内被这阵喧闹声惊醒，她们穿着睡衣和罩衫跑下楼。

"哦，父亲，我们又会成为富人了。"伊莉斯大叫起来。

"我们可以离开这讨厌的房子，搬回镇上住了。"克劳德说。

"我们将再次成为有钱、有身份的人了。"亨利满怀憧憬地大声说。

"父亲，给我们带回新衣服、新鞋子，还有新帽子。"雷内提出要求。

"See if you can bring some jewelry, too, won't you?" asked Elise.

"I'll see what I can do," their father promised.

Beauty did not ask for anything. She wondered if the money her father would receive could ever be enough to satisfy her sisters.

Noticing how quiet she had become, he asked, "What do you want, Beauty?"

"Perhaps just a rose, which is so hard to find here," she said. If she didn't ask for something, she thought, it would make her sisters angry.

"I'll see what I can do," he said, touching her cheek tenderly. Then, with the help of his sons, he prepared for his journey to town to meet with his lawyer.

"看你还能不能带些珠宝回来，行吗？"伊莉斯问。

"到时候如果情况允许，我会办到的。"她们的父亲答应了下来。

贝蒂没有要求任何东西，她怀疑父亲得到的钱能否满足两个姐姐的要求。

父亲注意到贝蒂一声不吭，于是问她："贝蒂，你想要什么呢？

"如果可以的话就给我带一朵玫瑰吧，这里很难见到的。"她说。她觉得，要是自己不向父亲要求点什么，会惹怒两个姐姐的。

"我知道了。"说着，他轻轻地抚摸贝蒂的脸颊。之后，在两个儿子的帮助下，他打点好一切，准备去镇上会见他的律师。

5

MORE DISAPPOINTMENTS

The seaside town was bustling with *activity*. Ships were docked and being loaded and unloaded by workmen and sailors. Merchants, tradesmen, and sailors were conducting their business, while townspeople and country folk milled about. Children ran through the streets between the horses and carts, grabbing on to their parents' hands so as not to get lost in the crowd.

When the merchant arrived, he went to see his lawyer.

"It is good to see you, sir," Beauty's father said, extending his hand to the lawyer. The man hardly looked up to acknowledge the merchant's presence.

"Good day to you," the lawyer muttered, frowning. "Although it won't be a day of good news for you, monsieur, I regret to say."

"What do you mean?" the merchant asked, taking the letter about his *merchandise* out of his pouch.

五

更大的失望

　　海滨小镇呈现出一片繁忙的景象。船只停靠码头后，工人和水手正忙着装卸货物。批发商、零售商和水手们正在岸边做买卖，镇上的居民和乡下来的人在街上四处走动。孩子们在车水马龙的大街上快速穿行，他们紧紧地抓住父母亲的手，才不至于在人群中走失。

　　商人来到镇上，立刻去见他的律师。

　　"很高兴见到您，先生。"贝蒂的父亲向律师伸出手，说道。对于商人的到来，律师几乎连头也没抬一下。

　　"日安，"律师眉头紧锁，嘟囔着说，"很抱歉，今天对你来说没什么好消息。"

　　"什么意思？"商人从口袋里掏出那封通知他货物抵达的信件，问道。

"The merchandise has finally arrived, but there is very little of it. It will be confiscated by creditors to whom you owe great sums of money," the lawyer responded. "It seems there is not enough money to pay off your debts. You are poorer than before."

"How can this be?" the merchant cried in despair.

"Come and take a seat and see what I've found," said the lawyer.

The merchant and the lawyer carefully went over all of the accounts. The lawyer said that the bulk of the merchandise was lost at sea, and customs agents and profiteers had stolen much of the rest of it. The merchant owed more money than he ever imagined.

The merchant thanked the lawyer for his help, and turned to leave.

"I will, of course, inform you if anything changes, monsieur," the lawyer assured him.

The merchant left town with a heavy heart. He wondered how he would explain this new disappointment to his children.

He knew that Beauty would make the best of it. He looked forward to her smiles and hugs upon his return. As for his other children, he knew that his sons would grumble but would be cheered by Beauty's good nature. His other daugh-

"货物倒是到了，可是量太少，会被你那些大债主没收的。"律师回答说，"看上去它还不够还清你的债务。现在你比以前更穷了。"

"怎么会这样呢？"商人绝望地哀号。
"过来坐下吧，看看我手头的资料。"律师说。

商人和律师仔细地查了一遍所有的账目。律师说，他的大部分货物在海上丢失了，剩余的大都被海关代理人和奸商侵吞。商人欠下的债务比他想象的还要多。

商人谢过律师，转身要走。

"如果出现转机，我一定会通知您的，先生。"律师说。

商人心情沉重地离开小镇，他想着该如何向孩子们解释这新的失望。

他知道，贝蒂会往好处想，他盼着回到家贝蒂微笑着拥抱他。至于其他孩子，他知道儿子对此会有所抱怨，不过会

ters would be a problem, and he feared that they would take out their resentment on Beauty.

"What am I to do?" he whispered, looking skyward. He hoped that on the journey home he would find the courage to face his family.

被贝蒂的乐观感染，重新振作起来。另外两个女儿可就麻烦了，他担心她们会把怒气发泄到贝蒂身上。

"我该怎么办？"他仰望天空，喃喃自语。他希望在回家的路上能够获得面对家人的勇气。

6

LOST IN THE WOODS

Weary from traveling for days, the merchant was very close to home and was looking forward to seeing his children in spite of his bad news. Then he got lost in the forest.

How often I've traveled this road, he thought as he came to a crossroads. "I am certain this is the way," he mumbled, pulling his horse's reins with fingers that were becoming numb from the cold.

An hour or so later, it seemed he had come to the same crossroads. "This is not possible!" he said, sighing with growing frustration as he led the horse in the other direction this time.

As he rode on, the weather changed. Snow and freezing rain fell mercilessly about him. The bitter cold made him shiver uncomfortably.

It was so windy that twice he fell off his horse, which continually lost its footing on the icy roads. Traveling was becoming more and more dangerous and the merchant more and more weary.

36

六
在森林里迷路

一连赶了几天的路，就快到家了。此时，商人疲惫不堪，尽管带回的是坏消息，他还是盼着早点见到孩子们。可就在这个时候，他在森林里迷路了。

他走到一个十字路口，心里想着，这条路我不知走了多少遍。"我确信就是这个方向。"他咕哝着，用快冻僵的手拉了拉缰绳。

大概过了一个小时，他好像又回到了刚才那个十字路口。"这不可能！"说着他让马朝着另一个方向前进，心中越来越沮丧，边走边叹气。

骑马前进的时候，天气发生了变化。雪花和冰冷的雨无情地落到他身上，严寒让他难受得直打哆嗦。

马在结冰的路面上经常失蹄，风也很大，刮得他两次跌落马背。这一路变得越来越艰险，商人也感到越来越疲倦。

When night fell, he wondered whether he would freeze to death or be lost so long in the woods that he would starve. When he heard wolves howling, he feared being eaten by them.

"I am doomed," he said, sighing. Clutching his horse's reins and gathering his coat and hat about him, he rode on for hours through the icy mist and swirling winds.

Suddenly there was a break in the trees. The merchant could see a path through the forest. As he rode along the path, the weather changed again. It was no longer windy, snowing, and cold, but becoming pleasantly warm.

Ah, perhaps there is a place to rest nearby, he thought hopefully.

In the distance there was light. He rode toward it, still hoping to find shelter. Soon he reached a courtyard that bordered a magnificent estate with a castle and stables and other smaller buildings around them.

The merchant entered the courtyard. The area was thoroughly lit, but no one was there to receive him.

夜幕降临的时候，他怀疑自己即使不被冻死，也会因为在森林里迷路太久而饿死。当他听见狼的嚎叫声时，又害怕被狼吃掉。

他叹了口气说："我命该如此。"他拽紧马缰，拉紧衣服和帽子，在冰冷的薄雾和旋风里跋涉了好几个小时。

树林在某处突然中断了。商人看见一条小路从森林穿过。当他骑马沿这条路前行时，天气又发生了变化。风住了，雪停了，天气不再寒冷刺骨，而是变得温暖宜人。

啊，或许附近有地方可以休息一下，他心中满怀希望。

远处有亮光！他朝亮光走去，心中一直盼着找一处避难所。很快，他来到一个院子，院子旁边是一座宏伟的建筑——有城堡、马厩，还有其他小的房子围绕其间。

商人走进院子。这地方灯火通明，但却没有人出来招待他。

7

THE GREAT CASTLE

Seeing the stable door open, the merchant directed his horse into it. The starving horse began to eat all of the hay and oats it could find.

"Poor beast," the merchant said. "I hope the master here doesn't mind."

The merchant secured the horse in the stable and walked toward the main building. It was a large palace with turrets and gargoyles decorating gables that pointed toward the sky.

Numerous statues stood in the courtyard leading to the castle. They were lifesize and lifelike, scattered in no particular design. They were all the same pale color, but each was dressed differently. Some appeared to be soldiers, some servants, and others nobility. The merchant hurried on since he was still cold from his trip.

He approached the doors of the palace and entered

七

宏伟的城堡

看见马厩的门开着，商人把马牵了进去。饿坏了的马把所有能找到的干草和燕麦往肚子里吞。

"可怜的家伙，"商人说，"希望这里的主人不会介意。"

商人在马厩里把马安置好，然后朝这里的主建筑走去。那是一座宏伟的宫殿，宫殿的塔楼和山形墙高耸入云，上面装饰着怪兽状的滴水嘴。

院子里立着无数的雕像，一直通往城堡。它们跟真人一般大小，栩栩如生，凌乱地散布在院子里。它们个个面色苍白，可是衣着各异：有些像是士兵，有些像是仆人，还有些像是贵族。一路上商人仍然觉着冷，所以他加快了脚步。

他来到宫殿门口，小心翼翼地走了进去。巨大的入口处

cautiously. The large entranceway was decorated with tapestries, candelabra, and rich furnishings. A gilded mirror covered one of the walls. As he walked past the mirror, he saw something reflected in it.

"Hello," he called, turning around quickly, but he saw no one. When he looked into the mirror a second time, he could only see his own reflection — a red-cheeked, shivering, stooped man badly in need of a fire, food, and a place to rest.

"Is anyone here?" he called out. His words echoed throughout the hall. Since there was no answer, he walked on and found a welcoming fire burning in the fireplace of a comfortable sitting room. To his suprise, he saw a table set for one, spread with a bountiful meal.

Although he was starving, at first he didn't want to help himself to the meal. Perhaps someone will come while I get warm, he thought as he moved as close to the fire as possible.

Hours later, still no one had come into the sitting room. The merchant was amazed that the fire still roared, never lessening to embers in all that time. Unbearably hungry, he sat down and dined on delicious chicken and other roasted meats. He enjoyed fresh fruits, sweets, and refreshing cool water. As he ate, he noticed how elegant everything in the palace was.

Why doesn't someone come? he wondered. He crossed

挂着织锦，摆着烛台，装饰得富丽堂皇。有一堵墙上挂着一面镀金的镜子。当他从镜子旁走过时，看见镜子里映出了什么东西。

"你好。"他赶紧转过身打招呼，可是并没看见什么人。当他再次朝镜子里看时，只见到自己的样子——脸颊通红、浑身哆嗦、佝偻着身子，急需炉火、食物和休息的地方。

"有人在吗？"他大声喊道，话音在大厅里回响。没有人回答他，于是，他继续朝前走，在一间舒适的起居室里找到了一处燃烧着的炉火，像是在欢迎他的到来。令人吃惊的是，他看见一张餐桌上面摆着丰盛的饭菜，是为一个人准备的。

尽管他已经饥肠辘辘，可是一开始他并不打算享用这顿美餐。或许当我身子暖和起来的时候会有人进来，他一边想，一边尽可能地靠近炉火。

几个小时过去了，始终不见有人来起居室。在这期间炉火居然一直烧得很旺，怎么烧都不灭，商人很是惊讶。他饥饿难耐，终于坐下来享用美味的鸡肉和其他各式烤肉，以及新鲜的水果、糖果和提神爽口的凉水。吃饭的时候，他发现宫殿里的一切都是如此雅致。

为什么没人出现呢？他感到好奇。他穿过大厅，走进几

the hall and entered several smaller apartments. Each apartment had exquisite furnishings, large mirrors, chandeliers, portraits, and fanciful murals that depicted sprites and fairies, mythological creatures, and kings and queens. As he walked through the entrance hall, he looked at the murals. In some of them the royals and fairies were engaged in sports and games. In others, the fairies and kings led armies and celebrated victories. Still others showed life at court where enchantment went hand in hand with daily life.

The merchant walked on and found a banquet hall, a ballroom, and many large bedchambers with sitting rooms. Since it was already quite late and he was exhausted, the merchant chose one of the bedchambers and settled down to sleep.

个小套间。每个套间里都摆放着精致的装饰品和大镜子，天花板上吊着枝状的装饰灯，墙上挂着画像，还刻有奇异的壁画，壁画上绘着鬼怪、精灵和神话中的人物，还有国王和王后。走过入口处的大厅时，他看着这些壁画——有些描绘皇室成员和精灵们一起运动、做游戏的场面；有些描绘精灵和国王率领军队庆祝胜利的场景；还有些描绘宫廷里充满魔法的日常生活。

　　商人继续朝前走，发现城堡里有一个宴会厅和一个舞厅，还有许多带着起居室的大卧房。这时，夜已经很深了，商人感到筋疲力尽，于是他挑了一间卧房，躺下来睡了。

8

THE NEXT MORNING

The merchant tossed and turned all night. He dreamed of his children and his unhappy meeting with the lawyer.

After such a fitful night's sleep, the merchant was surprised to wake and find that it was already late the next morning. The sun was shining into the bedchamber where he slept.

Even though he wanted to meet and thank whoever lived at the castle, he hoped to get an early start to return home to his children before dark. He rose abruptly to prepare to leave.

"What is this?" the merchant asked when he reached for his clothes. Near the bed where he slept were a new suit of clothes and a pair of fine boots to replace his own dirty, tattered suit and shoes. He climbed out of bed and picked up the jacket and trousers that hung over the wardrobe. I must be in the home of a fairy that has taken pity on me, he thought as he dressed in the new clothes.

八
第二天早上

一整晚，商人辗转反侧。他梦见自己的孩子，还梦见与律师那次不愉快的会面。

他断断续续地睡了一晚，醒来时惊奇地发现已是第二天晌午，太阳照进了他睡觉的卧房。

尽管他想见见住在这座城堡里的人，对他表示感谢，但是他更希望能够早点动身，赶在天黑以前到家，回到孩子们身边。他猛地站起身，准备离开。

"这是什么？"商人伸手拿衣服的时候问。在他睡过的床边放着一套崭新的衣服和一双漂亮的靴子，原来那肮脏、破烂的衣服和鞋子已经不见了。他从床上爬起来，从衣橱里挑了一件夹克和一条裤子。他穿上新衣服的时候心里想，我肯定是到了精灵的家里，受到了她的怜悯。

While dressing, he looked through a window and was able to see how *magnificent* the estate was. The snow and dark clouds of the previous evening had given way to blue skies and bright sun. Flower *arbors* and gardens with walking paths lined with orange trees stretched as far as he could see. This is amazing, he thought, taking it all in as he laced up the new boots.

Now more than ever he was convinced that he had come to a place that was under some kind of enchantment. He wondered about the murals he had seen the night before in the hallway.

He left the bedchamber. Passing the mirror, he stopped to admire his reflection in his new suit of clothes. As he walked away from the mirror, he saw something else momentarily reflected there from the corner of his eye. "What was that?" he asked aloud, looking into the glass again. Convinced it was nothing, he walked on.

Surprisingly, he had no trouble finding his way through the *labyrinth* of apartments that led back to the great hall and the small sitting room where he had dined the night before.

As if by magic, the table was set with a hot drink of cocoa and a light breakfast. "I can only thank you, my good fairies, for seeing to my needs again this morning," he said, raising his cup in a toast to the fairies in the mural and enjoying his meal.

穿衣的时候他朝窗外望去，才发现这地方有多么地宏伟。昨天晚上的大雪和乌云早已散去，现在天空湛蓝、阳光明媚。凉亭四周缀满鲜花，花园的小径两旁种着成排的橘树，一直延伸到他视线的尽头。太神奇啦，他注意到这一切，边束紧新靴子边想着。

现在他更加确信自己到了一个魔法之地。他对昨晚在走廊里看到的壁画感到惊讶。

他离开卧房，经过镜子时停了下来，欣赏身上的新衣服。离开镜子时，他的眼角刹那间瞥见镜子里映出了什么东西。"那是什么？"他大叫，再次朝镜中看去。等他确信什么都没有后，接着朝前走。

令人惊讶的是，他竟然轻易地穿过迷宫一般的房间，回到宽敞的大厅和昨晚用餐的小起居室。

好像变魔术似的，此时餐桌上放着一杯热可可，还有一份简单的早餐。"我只能对您表示感谢，仁慈的精灵，今天早上您再次顾及到我的需求。"说着，他举起杯子，朝壁画上的精灵祝酒，然后开始享用早餐。

9

THE BEAST

After breakfast, the merchant went to the stable for his horse. On his way, he passed a rose garden and remembered Beauty's humble request. He selected a branch on which there were several perfect blooms and broke it off the bush. "My Beauty will enjoy these," he said to himself as he admired the flowers and their fine scent.

"What is the meaning of this?" came a ferocious voice from right behind him. Hovering menacingly near the merchant stood a horrible Beast. The merchant nearly fainted from the shock of seeing such a huge creature. The Beast resembled a man, stood upright, and was well dressed but, nonetheless, was a monster.

"How ungrateful you are, sir!" the Beast said in a frightful voice. "Is this the thanks I get for welcoming you into my castle and for saving your miserable life? You steal what I value most in the world! You'll pay for it, I assure you."

九

野　兽

吃过早饭，商人来到马厩牵马。路上，经过玫瑰园时，他想起了贝蒂的小小请求。于是，他挑了一株盛开着几朵非常漂亮的玫瑰的花枝，把它折了下来。"我的贝蒂会喜欢的。"他欣赏着玫瑰，嗅着芬芳的花香，自言自语。

"你这么做算什么？"从他背后传来凶猛的声音。就在商人身边站着一头可怕的野兽。眼见这头庞然大物，商人吓得差点晕了过去。尽管野兽像人一样用双腿站立，而且打扮得很体面，可它毕竟是一头怪兽。

"先生，你是多么忘恩负义啊！"野兽的声音听起来很可怕，"我欢迎你来到我的城堡，把你从不幸中解救出来，难道你就这样答谢我吗？你偷走了我在这世上最珍贵的东西！我一定要让你为此付出代价。"

"Forgive me. Your Highness. I was taking a rose to one of my daughters," the merchant begged. He had fallen to the ground on his knees.

"Do not call me Your Highness. I do not want any important titles. I prefer to be called the Beast. Don't offer me false compliments, but just say what you think," he growled.

The merchant shook his head to acknowledge the Beast's words.

It took a few moments for the merchant to compose himself. Then he offered the Beast an honest explanation of why he wanted the rose.

"I meant no harm, sir. My dear daughter Beauty asked for nothing from my travels but a rose."

The Beast was curious about the girl and let the merchant continue.

"My other two daughters demanded things I could not hope to buy. You see, I lost my fortune and now I am penniless. I had traveled to town to see to my affairs, hoping to regain some small portion of my lost fortune," the weeping merchant continued.

The Beast listened with interest.

"饶恕我吧，阁下。我想带一朵玫瑰回去给我的一个女儿。"商人双膝跪倒在地，乞求道。

"别叫我'阁下'。我可不要什么头衔。我更喜欢被叫做野兽。别曲意奉承我，想到什么就直说吧。"他咆哮起来。

商人摇了摇头，听从了野兽的吩咐。

商人花了点时间让自己镇定下来。接着，他诚恳地向野兽解释为什么他想要玫瑰花。

"我并没有恶意，先生。我这次出门，亲爱的女儿贝蒂别无他求，只想我给她带一朵玫瑰花。"

野兽对他说到的这个女孩很好奇，让商人继续讲下去。

"其他两个女儿向我要求的东西我都不指望买得起。你瞧，我破产了，现在身无分文。我赶到镇上去看我的生意，希望能重新找回小部分丢失的财物。"商人哭了起来，接着说道。

野兽饶有兴致地听着。

"Please, kind sir, spare me. I can see that you are fair and generous."

"You cannot flatter me," the Beast said, "but I will forgive you and let you go, on one condition."

"What is that?" the merchant asked in a low, humbled voice.

"One of your daughters must come here in your place. She must come of her own choosing and be willing to give her life in exchange for your own," the Beast demanded.

"I can't do that!" the merchant exclaimed.

"You must, if you are to live. If your daughters refuse, you must return within three months and accept your fate," the Beast commanded.

"But I —" the merchant began.

"There is nothing more to say! Go on and swear you will return in three months if none of your daughters come in your place," the Beast bellowed.

"I swear," the merchant said, but he had no intention of sending any of his children to suffer in his place at the hands of the monster.

"Don't think you can fool me, old man," the Beast roared. "If you don't return I will come for you! Do you promise to return?"

"I do," the merchant repeated sadly. He would take this opportunity to return home and say good-bye to his children. Then he would return to the castle and accept his fate.

"Take a rose to Beauty and leave whenever it pleases you,"

"仁慈的先生，请您宽恕我。看得出来，您很公正、大度。"

"你没法讨好我，"野兽说，"我可以原谅你，并且让你离开，不过有个条件。"

"是什么条件？"商人用低沉、谦卑的口气问。

"你的一个女儿必须来这里顶替你。她必须出于自愿，并且肯拿自己来换取你的性命。"野兽说。

"我不能这么做！"商人大叫起来。

"如果你想活下去，就必须这么做。要是你的女儿拒绝，那么你必须在三个月以内赶回，接受你的命运。"野兽命令道。

"可是，我——"商人说。

"别废话！要是你的女儿都不愿顶替你，那么你发誓三个月内回到这里。"野兽怒吼。

"我发誓。"商人说，可是他并不想把任何一个孩子送到怪物手上，替他受苦。

"别想着愚弄我，老头，"野兽吼道，"要是你不回来，我就会出去找你！你发誓会回来吗？"

"我会的。"商人悲伤地重复着。他打算利用这个机会回家跟孩子们告别。之后，他就回到城堡，接受自己的命运。

"带一朵玫瑰给贝蒂，你随时可以离开了。"野兽说着，

the Beast said, giving a branch with the loveliest rose to the merchant. "But don't leave before first returning to the chamber where you slept. There is a large empty chest there. Fill it with whatever treasures you want and I will send it to your home."

Then the Beast left the merchant, who stood shaking in the courtyard, frightened and bewildered.

递给商人一枝最漂亮的玫瑰，"离开之前，去一下你睡过的房间。那里有一只很大的空箱。你可以往里面装任何你想要的财宝，我会把它送到你家。"

接着，野兽离开了。留下商人一个人站在院子里，惊恐而又迷惘，不住地发抖。

10

TREASURES FROM THE CASTLE

The merchant returned to the bedchamber as quickly as he could, fearing that at any moment the Beast would be upon him again. He closed the door of the room behind him just to be safe. Inside he found the chest and began to gather fine things to put into it. The room was filled with precious objects of every kind. In fact, the closets and shelves were now laden with treasures for the taking!

"At least I will be able to leave something to my children," the merchant muttered halfheartedly as he filled the chest with gold, silver, and jewels.

The chest seemed to be bottomless. No matter how much the merchant put into the chest, more fit into it. It seemed that it would be impossible for anyone to lift the chest. The merchant wondered if the Beast was mocking him and had no intention of sending the chest to his home.

十

城堡里的财宝

商人以最快的速度返回卧房,一路上担心野兽会再次出现。为了安全起见,他随手关上了房门。在卧房里面他找到了那口箱子,开始把好东西装进去。房里放满了各式各样的奇珍异宝。事实上,现在连壁橱和架子也满满地放着宝物,这些东西他都可以带走!

"至少我可以给孩子们留下点东西。"商人一边往箱子里塞金银珠宝,一边漫不经心地嘟囔着。

箱子好像个无底洞,不管商人往里面装多少东西,总还有地方空着。看这架势,不可能有人抬得动它。商人怀疑野兽在捉弄他,野兽根本不打算把这箱子送到他家去。

Nonetheless, he filled it as much as possible. Then he left the bedchamber and quietly walked through the hallways, hoping to avoid the Beast again. Carrying the rose, he returned to the stable to get his horse, which had been prepared for riding. He mounted his horse and rode through the courtyard, passing the curious collection of statues once again.

As he rode down the tree-lined path, the merchant was filled with grief. The haven he had sought and luckily found out of the storm had turned into a nightmarish trap, threatening to destroy his family and all that he held most dear. Once again, fate had dealt him a terrible blow.

The horse seemed to know its way and found a road that led through the icy mist and swirling winds that obscured the castle. The horse was through the forest and home in a few short hours.

即便如此，商人仍然尽可能地把东西往箱子里塞。然后，他离开卧房，悄悄地穿过走廊，希望别再遇见野兽。他带上玫瑰，回到马厩牵马，此时，他的马已经整装待发。他骑上马，穿过院子，再次经过那些奇怪的雕像群。

沿着绿树成荫的小路骑行时，商人心里充满了悲伤。他在暴风雨中有幸找到的这处避难所，竟然变成一个噩梦般的陷阱，威胁着要毁灭他的家庭以及他最珍爱的一切。命运再次给了他沉重的一击。

马儿似乎认识路。寒雾和旋风遮蔽了城堡，马儿在其中穿行，走出了森林。短短几个小时以后，他就回到了家里。

11

A BITTERSWEET REUNION

Finally, the merchant came to the edge of the field where his sons were working.

"Hello, Father!" Henri shouted.

"What news have you from town?" Claude asked eagerly, wanting to know if they were rich once again.

The merchant signaled them to meet him back at the house. As the merchant rode toward the cottage, his two sons raced each other across the field to see who would get there first.

The merchant brought his horse to the stable. After removing the saddle, halter, and reins he went into the house, where his eager sons already stood.

Elise and Rene were lounging in the sitting room when they saw their father's approaching horse. They ran to the door to greet him, but only after they had messed their hair and smudged their faces with coal from the fireplace to make it appear that they had been hard at work.

十一

悲喜交集的团圆

商人终于来到自家的田边,他的两个儿子正在田里干活。

"嘿,父亲!"亨利大叫起来。

"你从镇上带回了什么消息?"克劳德急切地问,想知道他们是不是又成了富人。

商人示意他们回家再说。当商人骑马朝自家的农舍走去时,他那两个儿子穿过田地,你追我赶,看谁先到家。

商人把马牵进马厩,卸下马鞍、笼头和缰绳后走进家门。两个急不可耐的儿子早就在家等候了。

伊莉斯和雷内正懒洋洋地在起居室里踱步,眼见父亲骑马回来,她们赶紧跑到门口去迎接他。当然,她们先弄乱自己的头发,又用火炉里的木炭把脸涂黑,为的是证明她们一直在辛勤地干活。

"Father is back!" Rene shouted.

"Look at the fine clothes he wears!" Claude observed, assured that his father had returned with good news.

"Welcome home. Father," Henri said warmly.

"Let's see what he has brought us," Elise added excitedly.

Beauty, who was setting logs in the fireplace, was the first to give her dear father a welcoming hug. Her affection was most genuine.

The merchant hugged each of his children, grateful to have returned to them. Then, sadly, he held out the rose. "Here, Beauty, this is for you. The price for it was very dear, indeed," he said, trying to hold back his tears.

"Father, what has happened?" Beauty asked, while her brothers helped the merchant into a chair.

"You will not believe what has befallen me," said the merchant anxiously as his children listened.

First, the merchant told his children about the disappointing meeting with the lawyer.

"So we are no better off than before," Henri said, sighing.

"No, we are worse off than before," moaned Claude while Elise's and Rene's smiles turned to frowns.

"Let me continue," said the merchant. Then he told them about getting lost in the forest during the terrible storm and finding the castle.

"父亲回来啦！"雷内大声叫着。

"瞧他穿得多考究啊！"克劳德经过一番观察，确信父亲带回来的是好消息。

"欢迎回家，父亲。"亨利热烈地说。

"我们来瞧瞧他给我们带回了什么东西。"伊莉斯激动地插话。

贝蒂当时正往火炉里添柴火，她第一个上去拥抱亲爱的父亲，欢迎他回来。她的感情最真挚。

商人同孩子们一一拥抱，庆幸又回到他们身边。接着，他伤感地拿出玫瑰花。"贝蒂，这是给你的。事实上，我为它付出了昂贵的代价。"他说着，忍住不让眼泪掉下来。

"父亲，发生了什么事？"贝蒂问。哥哥们把父亲扶到椅子上。

"你们不会相信发生在我身上的事情的。"孩子们听商人讲述的时候，他不安地说。

首先，商人告诉孩子们自己与律师那次令人失望的会面。

"这么说，我们还跟以前一样。"亨利叹了口气。

"不，我们比以前更加糟糕。"克劳德抱怨说。这时，伊莉斯和雷内脸上的笑容僵住了，皱起了眉头。

"听我把话说完。"商人说。接着，他告诉孩子们自己怎样遇上了恐怖的暴风雨，在森林里迷路，后来又怎样找到一座城堡。

"How lucky you were. Father, to find shelter on so horrible a night," said Elise while Rene nodded in agreement. In spite of their interruptions, the merchant went on. When he told them about meeting the Beast, they all gasped in horror.

"This is all your fault. Beauty!" Rene accused.

"How heartless you are not to even shed a tear," Elise added.

"It would never have happened if you hadn't asked for that ridiculous rose! Now that will be the death of our poor father," Rene hissed.

Claude and Henri stood by silently as their sisters tormented Beauty.

Beauty listened to their accusations, but didn't cry at all, even though she knew they were being unjust. Beauty knew what she had to do, and that was all that mattered to her.

"父亲，您多么幸运啊！能在这么可怕的夜晚找到一处避难所。"伊莉斯说，雷内点头表示赞同。商人没有理睬她们的插话，径直讲下去。当他说到遇见野兽的那段遭遇时，他们都吓得透不过气来。

"贝蒂，这都是你的错！"雷内责备她。

"你多么无情啊，居然连一滴眼泪都没有。"伊莉斯跟着说。

"假如你没向父亲要那朵荒唐的玫瑰，这一切就不会发生了。现在我们可怜的父亲就要死了。"雷内发出嘘声。

当姐妹俩折磨贝蒂的时候，克劳德和亨利默默地站在一旁。

贝蒂听着她们的责备，虽然心中清楚她们这么做不公平，可是却压根儿不哭。贝蒂知道自己该怎么做，对她来说，那才是最重要的。

12

BEAUTY'S DECISION

T he reason I am not crying is because Father won't die on my behalf," Beauty said firmly. "The Beast has asked for one of his daughters, and I will go to save Father's life. That is how much I truly love him," Beauty said.

Beauty's brothers suddenly stepped forward. "No, Beauty, it is not you or Elise or Rene or Father who will return to the Beast's castle. We will go," Claude said bravely.

"Yes, Claude and I will go there and kill the Beast, or die in the effort!" exclaimed Henri courageously.

"Why should any of us suffer for Beauty's folly?" Rene asked while Elise shook her head in agreement.

"That is impossible, my sons," the merchant said, wringing his hands.

"Then one of us will go in your place," Claude proposed.

"Yes," said Henri again strongly.

"There is no way to outdo the Beast. He has powers you cannot begin to imagine," their father said. "He would only

十二

贝蒂的决定

"我不哭是因为父亲不会为我而死。"贝蒂坚定地说，"野兽要父亲的一个女儿，那我就去救父亲的性命。我多么真切地爱着父亲。"贝蒂说。

贝蒂的两个哥哥突然走上前。"不，贝蒂，你，伊莉斯，雷内或者父亲都不要回野兽的城堡。我们去。"克劳德勇敢地说。

"是的，我和克劳德去那儿，把野兽杀死，或者战死！"亨利勇敢地说。

"为什么我们要为贝蒂的愚蠢承担后果？"雷内问。伊莉斯点头表示同意。

"儿子，那不可能。"商人搓着手说。

"那么我们其中一个去顶替你。"克劳德提议。

"是的。"亨利再次有力地说。

"不可能打败野兽的，他的能耐你们没法想象，"他们的父亲说，"他只接受我承诺过的以女儿作为交换。我已经

accept my promise of sending a daughter. I am old and have lived a long life. My only regret is not being able to spend the rest of my days with all of you. I will return to the castle in three months as I promised I would. I cannot accept Beauty's selfless offer, and I will not sacrifice my sons to the whims of this creature."

Beauty was deep in thought, overwhelmed by all that was happening. "Father," she said resolutely, "you may go to the castle. But you cannot stop me from following you there. I will accompany you one way or the other, since it was my wish for a rose that put you in this dreadful situation."

Beauty's father and brothers tried to convince her to change her mind, but she would not listen to them. Only her sisters rejoiced at the thought of her *imprisonment* in the Beast's castle, since they were so jealous of her.

Later that evening when the merchant went into his bedroom, he saw the chest filled with treasures sent from the Beast's castle. Until that moment, he had forgotten about it.

"The Beast has kept his word, and so I must keep mine when the time comes," he said sadly.

At first he decided not to tell his children about the chest because they would want to return to town if they thought they were again very rich. He wanted to remain in the country. He called Beauty into his room and entrusted her with his secret.

老了，也活得够长了。唯一遗憾的是，我没法与你们一起度过余生。三个月后我就回到城堡，兑现我的诺言。我不能接受贝蒂无私的奉献，也不会为了怪物一时的兴致牺牲我的儿子。"

贝蒂陷入了沉思，她被眼前发生的一切所震撼。"父亲，"她果断地说，"您可以去城堡，但是您没法阻止我跟您一起去。不管怎样我都会陪着您，都是我想要一朵玫瑰，才让您陷入这么可怕的境地。"

贝蒂的父亲和哥哥都想说服她改变主意，可是，她不想听他们的劝告。只有她那两个姐姐，一想到她将被囚禁在野兽的城堡里就兴高采烈，因为她们是那么地嫉妒她。

那天夜深的时候，商人走进他的卧房，看见那口装满珍宝的箱子从野兽的城堡里送了过来。直到那一刻，他才想起这件事。

"野兽信守诺言，那么时间一到，我也要遵守我的承诺。"商人悲痛地说。

一开始，他决定不告诉孩子们关于箱子的事，因为如果他们知道自己又有钱了，就想搬回镇上住。但是，他想继续留在乡下。他把贝蒂叫到自己房里，与她分享自己的秘密。

"Beauty, look at what the Beast sent home with me," he said, lifting handfuls of gold, silver coins, and gems from its depths. Beauty could not believe her eyes.

"We must keep this hidden from your brothers and sisters for the time being," he said.

Beauty told her father that gentlemen had been calling on Elise and Rene. She did not resent her sisters and truly wished them happiness. So she told her father that it would be best to let them have their fortunes and be married. The merchant saw the wisdom in this and agreed.

At the end of three months. Beauty and her father prepared for the journey to the Beast's castle. Rene and Elise had their fortunes and would soon be married, and her brothers would stay in the country for the time being.

Before parting from their sister, Elise and Rene rubbed their eyes with *onions* to fake tears. "Oh, dear sister, how we'll miss you," Elise moaned dramatically.

"Be careful, dear Beauty," Rene said, sighing halfheartedly.

Beauty's brothers hugged her warmly and wished her and their father a safe journey and eventual return to their home.

Bravely, Beauty did not express sorrow at the thought of what her future held. She didn't want to add to her family's anxiety — or her own.

"贝蒂，瞧瞧野兽给我们送来了什么。"说着，他从箱子底下抓起一把把金币银币，还有珠宝。贝蒂简直不敢相信自己的眼睛。

"眼下，我们必须对你的哥哥姐姐保守这个秘密。"他说。

贝蒂告诉父亲，在他离开的这段时间，一直有绅士来拜访伊莉斯和雷内。她并不憎恨姐姐，并且真诚地希望她们过得快乐。所以，她告诉父亲，最好让她们得到财产，能够找个人嫁出去。商人认为这是个明智的办法，于是同意了。

三个月期限就要到了，贝蒂和父亲准备前往野兽的城堡。雷内和伊莉斯得到了她们的财产，很快就会嫁人，她的两个哥哥暂时仍待在乡下。

雷内和伊莉斯在和妹妹告别的时候，用洋葱擦眼睛，挤出眼泪来。"哦，亲爱的妹妹，我们会多么想念你啊。"伊莉斯假装呜咽着。

"保重，亲爱的贝蒂。"雷内一边说，一边虚情假意地叹气。

贝蒂的两个哥哥热情地拥抱她，祝她和父亲一路平安，最终能够安全归来。

想到自己前途未卜，贝蒂并没有表现出悲伤来，而是十分勇敢。她不想给家人，也不愿给自己增添焦虑。

13

BEAUTY GOES TO THE BEAST'S CASTLE

Beauty and her father left the farm and took the road toward town. After traveling for hours, the horses, which seemed to know the way, turned onto a path that led to the palace. As had happened before when the merchant was lost in the forest, they left the icy mist and swirling winds and entered a tree-lined path where flowers bloomed as if it were spring. In the distance, they could see the palace illuminated as if in anticipation of their arrival.

"What kind of place is this. Father?" Beauty asked.

"One of unbelievable enchantment, Beauty, and of an unknown future," the merchant said somberly as he led the way.

Beauty and her father dismounted from their horses. As they walked toward the palace they passed the statues that lined the courtyard. Beauty felt that the statues were watching her. Although the statues were clearly made of stone, their faces were eerily lifelike. Beauty shivered when she looked at them.

十三

贝蒂前往野兽的城堡

贝蒂和父亲离开农庄，走上通往镇上的大道。他们的马好像认识路，经过几个小时的行程，他们走上了一条通往宫殿的小路。就像之前商人在森林里迷路一样，他们走出了寒雾和旋风，来到一条绿树成荫的小路。那里开满了鲜花，就像到了春天。远远的，他们可以看见城堡里灯火通明，好像野兽料到了他们会来。

"父亲，这是个什么样的地方？"贝蒂问。

"一个令人难以置信的充满魔法的地方，贝蒂，也是一个前途未卜的地方。"商人一边在前面带路，一边低沉地说。

贝蒂和父亲下了马。他们朝宫殿走去的时候，经过排列在院子里的雕像。贝蒂觉得这些雕像在盯着她看。尽管它们很明显是用石头做的，可是它们的脸看上去阴森恐怖。贝蒂看着它们的时候直哆嗦。

Beauty admired the lovely flower arbors as their horses went into the stable. Then Beauty's father led her into the great hall.

Following her father, Beauty had just come into the hall and was passing the mirror when she turned to look into it. She saw a fleeting image there — as if someone else, a handsome young man, were passing the mirror with her and escorting her into the castle. She looked more closely. Seeing nothing, she thought she was just tired from the long trip. She rubbed her eyes and caught up with her father.

"Father, did you see..." she began to ask but he moved ahead quickly to go into the sitting room.

"Beauty, look at the table! Again it is set for a feast — this time for two," said the merchant. "I have no appetite, though," he added sadly as he sat down in one of the brocade chairs.

Strangely, Beauty was amused by this. The Beast intends to fatten me up before making a meal of me, she thought. Not wanting to upset her father more than he already was, she put the thought out of her head and prepared a plate for him and then one for herself.

"Surely this is meant for us," said Beauty as she took a seat at the table. They ate quietly until they heard a ferocious growl that echoed through the palace.

他们把马牵到马厩的时候,贝蒂对凉亭里的花儿赞叹不已。接着,贝蒂的父亲带着她走进宏伟的大厅。

贝蒂跟着父亲走进大厅,经过一面镜子前,她朝镜子里看了一眼。她看到有个人影一闪而过——好像有什么人,似乎是一个英俊的年轻人跟着她一起经过镜子,护送她进入城堡。她近距离地朝镜子里看,没有发现任何东西,所以她想可能是长途奔波产生的幻觉。她揉了揉眼睛,追上了父亲。

"父亲,你有没有看见……"她问父亲,可他在前面快步走进了一间起居室。

"贝蒂,瞧餐桌上!又摆好了饭菜——这次准备了两份。"商人说,"可是我没胃口。"他又伤心地补充了一句,坐到一张套着织锦的椅子上。

奇怪的是,贝蒂觉得这一切很有趣。她想,原来野兽想把我养胖再吃掉。父亲已经很烦了,她不想再给他增添烦恼。于是,她打消了这个念头,给父亲准备了一个碟子,又给自己准备了一个。

"这当然是为我们准备的。"贝蒂说着在餐桌前的位子上坐了下来。他们不声不响地用餐,直到听见凶猛的咆哮声回荡在宫殿里。

"This is the end. Beauty," said the merchant in tears, fearing the worst. "The Beast has come!"

The Beast's face and figure terrified poor Beauty, but she tried not to show her feelings when he came and stood near her at the table.

"I am the Beast," he said harshly, introducing himself.

"I am Beauty," was her whispered response.

"Have you come of your own free will?" he asked Beauty.

"Yes, I have," she said, trembling as she uttered the words.

"And do you know that once your father leaves, you must stay here with me?" he questioned.

"Yes, it is my choice to do so," Beauty answered as calmly as she could.

The Beast seemed pleased with Beauty's response and moved toward the merchant's chair.

"Thank you, sir," the Beast said. "You are an honorable man. You must leave here tomorrow morning and never return. Before you leave, fill the chests in your bedchamber with whatever you want to take back to your family in remembrance of Beauty. Good night, Beauty. Farewell, good man." The Beast abruptly left the room.

Beauty bowed her head and whispered, "Good night, Beast."

"贝蒂，一切都结束了。"商人说着泪流满面，担心最糟糕的事情就要发生了，"野兽来了！"

当野兽走过来站在餐桌旁时，他的脸和身形吓坏了可怜的贝蒂，可是，她尽力抑制住害怕的情绪。

"我就是野兽。"他用严厉的口气介绍自己。
"我是贝蒂。"她轻声地回答。
"你是不是自愿来这里的？"他问贝蒂。
"是的，我是自愿的。"她说话的时候在发抖。
"那么你知不知道一旦你父亲离开，你就得跟我待在这里？"他问。
"是的，是我自己选择这么做的。"贝蒂回答的时候尽量让自己镇定。

看起来野兽对贝蒂的回答很满意，接着，他朝商人坐着的椅子走去。

"先生，谢谢你，"野兽说，"你是个诚实的人。明天一早你必须离开这里，永远不准回来。在你离开之前，去你睡过的卧房，把任何你想带回去的东西装进箱子里，为了纪念贝蒂。晚安，贝蒂。再见，好人。"说着，野兽突然离开了房间。

贝蒂低着头，轻声说："晚安，野兽。"

"Oh, Beauty!" the merchant cried when the Beast was gone. "You must not stay here! I can't leave you. You must go home and let me stay."

"No, Father, tomorrow morning you will leave and my fate will be in the hands of the Beast. Don't worry," Beauty assured him in a careful, determined tone. "I will be fine."

The merchant shook his head in resignation.

"哦，贝蒂！"等野兽走后，商人大叫起来，"你不准待在这里！我不会把你留下的。你必须回家，让我留下来。"

"不，父亲，明天早上你就离开这里，我的命运就交到野兽手里。别担心。"贝蒂慎重而坚定地向他保证，"我会没事的。"

商人无奈地摇摇头。

14

A SAD FAREWELL

Beauty and her father dreaded the onset of night and the inevitable coming of morning that would separate them forever. For the rest of the day they tried to enjoy each other's company and remain cheerful, despite the heavy cloud that hung over them.

Beauty looked around the great hall. Like her father, she was captivated by the murals of magical fairies, mythological creatures, and royalty.

The Beast did not appear, and that helped put Beauty and her father more at ease.

Later that evening. Beauty helped her father fill the chests that were in the same bedroom where he had slept during his first visit. At first, Beauty selected magnificent gowns, shoes, and hats for her sisters and fine suits, coats and boots for her brothers. But when her father opened a cabinet that was filled with gold and silver coins and jewels, she removed the clothing.

十四
伤感的离别

贝蒂和她父亲害怕夜晚的降临,害怕第二天早上不可避免的到来，那时他们将永远分开。在这一天剩余的时间里，两人尽量相依相伴、快快乐乐，尽管他们心底愁云密布。

贝蒂环顾整个大厅。像父亲一样，她也被墙上绘有魔法精灵、神话人物、皇室成员的壁画吸引住了。

野兽没再出现，这让贝蒂和父亲感到自在不少。

夜晚，贝蒂帮助父亲往箱子里装珍宝。箱子依然放在他第一次来时睡过的卧房里。起初，贝蒂为姐姐挑选华丽的礼服、鞋子和帽子，为哥哥挑选漂亮的衣服、外套和靴子。可是，当父亲打开装满金银珠宝的柜橱时，她又把衣服从箱子里拿了出来。

"Father," she said wisely, "it will be better for you to have coins that you can use readily. Then you can sell the jewels as you need to."

"Yes, Beauty, that will be best," he agreed. But the more they put into the chest, the more room there was in it. So, in the end, Beauty was able to include the fine clothing with the coins and jewels after all.

"The Beast is again very generous," the merchant said, sure this time that he would find the chests when he returned home. It would be more than enough to live on for the rest of his life.

"Beauty, this is not worth the price of losing you to the Beast and an unknown future," the merchant said.

"Don't worry, Father, I am sure everything will work out for the best," Beauty said, not wanting to alarm him.

Then the merchant retired to go to sleep. Beauty selected another room and went quietly into it after bidding her father good night.

Once they were settled in their rooms and comfortable in their beds, they slept soundly, surprisingly so, for the entire night.

While Beauty slept, she dreamed. In her dream, a lady dressed in fine clothes appeared to her.

"父亲，"贝蒂明智地说，"金币银币对你来说更好，你可以随时使用。必要的时候，你还可以变卖珠宝。"

"是的，贝蒂，这么做最好。"他表示同意。可是，他们往箱子里塞得越多，里面的空间就越大。所以，最后贝蒂把许多漂亮的衣服连同金银珠宝一起放进箱子里。

"野兽还是很慷慨。"商人说，并且确信这次回家就能见到这几口箱子。这些财宝足够他过完下半辈子。

"贝蒂，让你留在野兽身边，前途未卜，与此相比，这些东西又算得了什么呢。"商人说。

"别担心，父亲，我敢肯定一切都会好起来的。"贝蒂并不想让父亲担惊受怕。

接着，商人去睡觉了。贝蒂跟父亲道了声晚安，然后挑了另一间卧房，悄悄地走进去。

他们各自回到卧房，舒舒服服地躺在床上，奇怪的是，他们一整晚都睡得很香。

贝蒂睡着的时候做了个梦，梦中出现了一位衣着华丽的女士。

"Beauty, you have a good heart," the lady said. "By sacrificing your life to save your father's you have shown me a strong will, too. Your actions will be rewarded if you follow your heart."

The next morning when Beauty woke, she told her father about her dream and that the lady in it looked like one of the fairies in the murals in the great hall. Beauty was puzzled by the dream and its meaning.

"I hope your dream foretells good fortune," her father said, wishing the lady in Beauty's dream was the fairy he thought had seen to his needs during his first visit. Perhaps she would look after his daughter as well.

They walked arm in arm to the stable without encountering the Beast. Once again, the merchant found his horse equipped with provisions, saddled, and ready for the journey home.

The merchant cried when he and his beloved Beauty finally had to part.

After watching her father ride down the courtyard path and disappear in the distance. Beauty returned to the great hall. At first she sat at the fireside table and cried. Although she had kept her true thoughts from her father. Beauty was certain that the Beast would devour her that night.

"贝蒂，你有一颗善良的心，"这位女士说，"而且你牺牲自己来换取你父亲的性命，也说明你意志坚强。如果你遵照内心的指引行事，最终会获得回报。"

第二天早上，贝蒂醒来时把这个梦说给父亲听，她说，梦中的女士看上去就像大厅壁画上的一位精灵。贝蒂对这个梦和它的寓意迷惑不解。

"希望你的梦预示着好运。"她父亲说，并且盼望贝蒂梦中的这位女士就是他第一次来时照料他的精灵。或许她也会照料他的女儿。

他们手挽着手来到马房，一路上没有遇见野兽。商人再次发现他的马已经戴好马具，准备好上路回家。

当他和疼爱的贝蒂最后不得不分别的时候，商人流下了眼泪。

看着父亲骑马走在院子里的小路上直至消失在远方，贝蒂才回到大厅。她坐到壁炉边的桌子旁开始痛哭起来。其实贝蒂一直忍着没有把真实的想法告诉父亲，她确信野兽当晚就会吃掉她。

Mustering her courage, she decided to make the most of the time she had left and resolved to be strong. Then her thoughts turned to exploring the castle.

后来，她鼓起勇气，决定充分利用剩余的时间，变得坚强起来。接着，她想要探索一下这座城堡。

15

BEAUTY'S ROOM

Beauty discovered that the palace was filled with all kinds of wonders. The castle was very pleasant and warmly welcoming, in spite of its size, which stretched into two wings extended from the main building. She wandered through some of the grand rooms and then the smaller apartments.

She felt that it would take months for her to see all of its *splendors*, and wondered how much time she would have to explore it all.

In one part of the palace, she found an apartment with a sign over the door that read, "Beauty's Room."

Beauty approached the huge door. To open it she had to take the great gilded knob in both hands and pull with all her strength. She was surprised to see the elegance of the rooms before her. The chamber contained a *library* with books on floor-to-ceiling shelves. The ceiling was vaulted with windows that let the sun's natural light fill the room. It was very

十五
贝蒂的房间

贝蒂发现这座宫殿到处都是奇迹。城堡令人赏心悦目，而且有宾至如归的感觉，尽管它的面积实在很大——从主建筑物向两侧伸展，就像长出两个翅膀。她在几个宽敞的房间里闲逛，然后又参观了小一点的套间。

她觉得自己得花上几个月时间才能欣赏完所有的奇观，不过她不清楚自己到底还剩多少时日。

在宫殿的某个地方，她发现有个套间门口挂着一块牌子，上面写着"贝蒂的房间"。

贝蒂朝这扇巨大的房门走去。她不得不用双手握住很大的镀金门把手，使尽全身力气才把房门打开。她对眼前房内高雅的陈设深感惊讶。里面有一个藏书室，书架从地面伸展到天花板。玻璃制成的天花板成拱形，阳光可以洒满整个房

comfortable and spacious. The library consisted of thousands of books, and she was eager to look over its contents.

Another room in the apartment contained many musical instruments, all of which she could play. Beauty noticed a *harp*, which was her favorite instrument since she could play it and sing at the same time. Unlike the one at home that she often played to the delight of her father and brothers, this one was made of gold and decorated with diamonds and rubies.

There is so much here to keep my mind off of my fate, Beauty thought. If the Beast meant to harm me, then all of these *amusements* would not have been prepared for me, she reasoned. These thoughts gave her a renewed sense of comfort and courage.

Then Beauty went into the bedroom, where there was a large canopied bed with plush pillows. In the corner of the cozy room a warm fire welcomed her.

Picking up a book from the bedside table, she sat in a cushioned chair and opened the book to read. An inscription written in gold said:

Welcome Beauty, abandon fear,
You are queen and ruler here.
Name your wishes, say your will,
Each desire we will fulfill.

间。房间又舒服又宽敞。藏书室有数以千计的书，她急着想浏览一下书目。

另一间房里放着许多乐器，这些乐器贝蒂都会弹奏。贝蒂看到一架竖琴，这是她最喜爱的乐器，因为她能边弹边唱。她在家里经常弹竖琴，让父亲和哥哥开心，可是这架竖琴跟家里的不同，它是金子做成的，而且镶满了钻石和红宝石。

贝蒂心想，这里的东西可真多啊，让我不再去想自己的命运。她推想，如果野兽想要伤害我，那就没必要为我准备这些好玩的东西。这些想法让她重新得到了安慰和勇气。

接着，贝蒂走进卧房，那里摆着一张有罩盖的大床，床上还有毛茸茸的枕头。在舒适的房间一角，还有温暖的炉火迎接她。

贝蒂从床头柜上捡起一本书，坐到有垫子的椅子上，翻开书读了起来。题记是用烫金的字写的：

欢迎您贝蒂，请不要害怕，
您是这里的女王和统帅啊，
尽管说您的想法和意愿吧，
每个心愿我们都会实现它。

Is it possible that this, too, is meant for me? Beauty wondered. Does the Beast have the power to read my mind and satisfy my wishes? It seems to be so.

Beauty held the book near her heart and thought about her future and how it would *unfold* at the Beast's castle.

难道这也是在说我吗？贝蒂惊讶不已。难道野兽有能力读懂我的想法、满足我的心愿？好像是这么回事。

贝蒂把书捧在胸口，想着她的未来，思考着怎样在野兽的城堡里生活下去。

16

VISIONS

Puzzled by the words of the verse, Beauty wished more than anything that she could see her father. She turned toward the large mirror that stood near the dressing table and gasped. Reflected there was an image of her father Just as he was returning home. Beauty's heart leaped with joy to see this image, but then it broke to see her father look so sad.

He greeted his children and handed the horse's reins to his sons. Elise and Rene tried to look concerned, but it was obvious that they were glad that Beauty had not returned with their father. Beauty blinked a tear from her eye. When she looked again at the mirror the vision was gone.

Beauty found some comfort in the Beast's willingness to please her with this vision.

Before lunch. Beauty had time to wander through more of the rooms of the palace. There was a sewing room with materials and ribbons of every color and fabric and tools for needlework and other crafts.

十六

幻　影

　　贝蒂对这首诗迷惑不解，她现在最盼望能够见到父亲。她转过身，面向梳妆台旁边的大镜子，一下子屏住了呼吸。镜子里映现出她父亲，此时他正回到家里。看到父亲的样子后，贝蒂的心快乐得怦怦跳，可是，等看清父亲神色悲伤后，她又心如刀绞。

　　他向孩子们问好，然后把马缰递给儿子。伊莉斯和雷内拼命装出一副关切的模样，可是很明显，她们很高兴贝蒂没有跟父亲一起回来。贝蒂眼里闪着泪光。当她再次朝镜子里看时，影像消失了。

　　贝蒂从野兽为了讨好她而呈现的影像中得到了一些安慰。

　　午饭前，贝蒂还有时间参观宫殿里更多的房间。城堡里有一个缝纫间，里面有各种颜色、各种布料的带子和原料，以及做针线活和其他手工活所需的工具。

What lovely dresses I could make for Elise and Rene, she thought to herself, holding up a bolt of colorful silk and a handful of pearl buttons. Or a warm coat for father and trousers for Claude and Henri, she mused, seeing supplies of wool fabric.

A loom stood in one corner of the room near a window that overlooked a lovely flower garden. Beauty noticed the loom and recalled her own modest loom at home and the joy she had felt weaving at it.

How strange that everything here seems made just to please me, she thought, remembering the verse from the book as she walked toward the loom.

Passing another mirror that was near the loom, she saw a wavering image. The harder she tried to perceive the image, the more difficult it became.

Finally, the image became steady enough for her to make out a handsome young man — the same man she had seen on the evening of her arrival at the palace. He was standing near a majestic woman. Who are these phantoms? Beauty wondered.

The image faded quickly, and Beauty moved on in her explorations.

At noon, Beauty returned to the sitting room where she

她捧起一块彩色的丝绸，抓起一把珍珠纽扣，心想，我可以用它们为伊莉斯和雷内做漂亮的衣服啊！当看见羊毛织物的时候，她又琢磨着可以给爸爸做暖和的外套，给克劳德和亨利做保暖的裤子。

房间的角落里放着一台织布机，靠着窗户，从那里可以眺望漂亮的花园。贝蒂注意到它，不由得想起自己家里那台简陋的织布机，还有织布时的快乐心情。

多奇怪啊，这里的一切仿佛都是为了讨我的欢心！贝蒂向织布机走去时心里想，同时记起书上看到的那首小诗。

她经过织布机旁的另一面镜子时，看见一个摇晃不定的影像。她越是想看清楚，它就越是显得模糊。

最后，影像终于稳定下来，贝蒂看出这是一个英俊的小伙子——跟刚到这里的那天晚上在宫殿看到的是同一个人——他站在一个威严的女人身边。贝蒂很想知道，这些幻影到底是谁呢？

影像很快就隐去了，贝蒂继续在宫殿里探索。

中午，贝蒂回到她和父亲一起吃过早餐的起居室，她是

and her father had eaten breakfast. She was drawn there by the sound of music. Dinner was set upon the table. Beauty heard lovely music drifting through the room, but there were neither instruments nor musicians playing them.

How puzzling this is, she thought as she sat down to eat lunch. Remembering her father's belief that the palace was under an enchantment, she began to believe it herself.

被乐声吸引到那里的。午餐已经摆放在桌上了。贝蒂听见美妙的音乐在房间里萦绕，可是，那里既不见乐器，也看不到乐手演奏。

17

坐下来吃午饭的时候，贝蒂心想，这多么令人费解啊！她想起父亲坚信这座宫殿受魔法控制，现在，她也开始相信了。

17

AN EVENING TOGETHER

B eauty returned to her apartment to rest. She fell asleep and dreamed of the handsome young man.

"Beauty," he said to her softly, "help me win my freedom."

When Beauty woke she could not make sense of the dream.

She had neither seen nor heard the Beast all day. It seemed that they were entirely alone at the palace — or were they? Who is the handsome young man? Where is he? she wondered. Perhaps he is being held against his will some-where in the palace?

She rose from her nap to find the wardrobe in her room filled with lovely gowns, elegant shoes, and *precious* jewelry. Knowing they were meant for her, she selected a gown, dressed, and went to the main dining room for supper.

Then she heard a *ferocious* growl signaling the Beast's

十七

晚上的碰面

贝蒂回到自己的房间休息。她睡着了，梦见一个英俊的小伙子。

"贝蒂，"他温柔地对她说，"帮我获得自由。"

贝蒂醒来后，猜不透梦的寓意。

一整天她都没有看见野兽的踪影，也没听见他的声音。仿佛整个宫殿里独独他们两个存在——是这样的吗？那个英俊的小伙子是谁呢？他在哪里？她想知道答案。或许他正被囚禁在宫殿的某个地方？

打完瞌睡后她站起身，发现房间的衣柜里放满了漂亮的衣服、精致的鞋子和贵重的珠宝。她知道这些都是为她准备的，于是她挑了一件衣服穿上，然后就去主餐厅用晚餐。

接着，她听见一声凶猛的咆哮，这预示着野兽要出现

appearance. Although her spirits had lifted throughout the day as she viewed all of the splendors contained in the palace, Beauty's heart sank when she heard him approaching. Suddenly, she was afraid again.

"Beauty," the Beast asked, "can I watch you while you dine?" He came closer to her chair.

"Yes if that is your wish," Beauty answered, trying to remain calm as she placed portions of the fine meal on her plate.

"You rule here, Beauty. You alone can permit me to stay or send me away if my appearance troubles you," the Beast continued. "I will leave with haste if you desire it. Do you find me to be *ugly*?" he asked bluntly.

"I cannot lie to you. Beast," Beauty said. "You are unbecoming, but you seem to be good-natured," she said, sensing now that he meant her no harm.

"Yes," the Beast said. "I am ugly. I am not well spoken or intelligent. I am a simple, dimwitted Beast."

"You may not be lovely to look at, Beast, but you have the gift of self-reflection," Beauty said. "That proves to me that you are neither simple nor dimwitted."

The Beast stood steadily beside Beauty. "Enjoy your supper, Beauty," he said. "Know that everything in the palace is yours to enjoy and be amused by. If you are not happy here, I will be miserable."

了。白天贝蒂亲眼看见宫殿里各种奇观，精神振作了不少。可是，听见野兽来临，她的心又沉了下去。这一刻，她觉得害怕起来。

"贝蒂，"野兽问，"我能看着你用餐吗？"他走到贝蒂坐的椅子旁。

"可以，如果你想这么做的话。"贝蒂回答。她正把肉放到盘子里，说话时尽量让自己保持镇静。

"贝蒂，你是这里的主宰。你有权力让我留下来，要是我的样子让你感到不安，你也可以打发我离开。"野兽接着说，"要是你希望这么做的话，我会赶紧离开。你觉得我长得丑吗？"他直截了当地问。

"野兽，我没法对你说谎。"贝蒂说，"你的样子确实不好看，可是你看起来性情和善。"她说。现在她感觉到野兽对她没有恶意。

"是的，"野兽说，"我长得丑，而且笨嘴笨舌，又不聪明。我只是一头愚笨的野兽。"

"野兽，或许你的外表并不讨人喜欢，可是你善于自省。"贝蒂说，"在我看来，那证明你并不简单，也不愚笨。"

野兽一直站在贝蒂身边。"贝蒂，请用餐。"他说，"要知道，宫殿里的一切你都可以尽情享用。如果你在这里不开心，我会感到痛苦的。"

"Beast, thank you for your kindness. Please don't be sad. Your ugliness seems insignificant in light of your gentle manner," Beauty said. She was grateful for the tenderness of his words and his concern for her happiness.

"Yes, I do have a good heart," the Beast said, "but I am still a hideous monster."

Beauty thought carefully about the Beast's words. "Beast," she said, "many men are pleasing to the eye but brutal and more deserving of the name of Beast." "I prefer you to those whose good looks conceal a wicked heart," she said.

"If only I were clever enough to return a compliment for your kind words. I can only thank you plainly and offer my alle-giance to you, Beauty," the Beast said, sighing, as Beauty finished her meal.

Beauty lowered her head. She was touched by the Beast's kindness and humility. She wished she could feel more comfortable in his presence.

As she learned more about him, she began to trust that she had nothing to fear, even if his looks still terrified her. With time, she hoped, his looks would no longer be a barrier to their growing friendship.

"野兽，感谢你的好意，请别难过。与你的文雅举止相比，你的丑显得微不足道。"贝蒂说。她感激野兽言语体贴而且关心她是否快乐。

"是的，我确实有颗善良的心。"野兽说，"可我仍然是让人惊骇的怪兽。"

贝蒂仔细想了想野兽的话。"野兽，"她说，"许多人外表看起来赏心悦目，可是残酷无情，他们更适合被称做野兽。""比起那些外表好看、内心邪恶的家伙，我更喜欢你。"她又说。

"承蒙你看得起我，我实在不知道该如何表达谢意。我只能谢谢你，愿为你效劳，贝蒂。"野兽说，当贝蒂用完餐时，野兽叹了口气。

贝蒂低下头，她被野兽的善良和谦卑打动了。她真希望自己在野兽面前可以更加自在一些。

随着对野兽了解的加深，贝蒂开始相信她没什么好惧怕的，即使野兽的样子仍然让她恐惧。她希望随着时间的流逝，野兽的外表不再是他俩友谊不断加深的障碍。

18

THE FIRST PROPOSAL

The more she got to know the Beast, the more comfortable Beauty felt in his presence. Although his appearance was frightening, he was kind, gentle, and generous. Each evening, the Beast asked her to tell him how she had spent her day, and they talked about the many things that she had encountered at the palace. Soon she learned that his tone, which was threatening and ferocious, was due to his awkward, bulky size and not his nature.

"Was everything to your liking?" the Beast would ask.
"Unbelievably so," Beauty would answer.

They would talk for some time longer. Beauty spoke of her life at home with her father, sisters, and brothers, while the Beast listened intently but without saying very much. The conversation was polite but not engaging. The Beast asked simple questions only, ones that required simple answers. That is, until he suddenly asked, "Will you marry me, Beauty?" Beauty nearly fainted.

十八

第一次求婚

贝蒂对野兽了解得越多，在他面前就越是自在。尽管他外表吓人，可是心地善良、举止温柔、慷慨大方。每天晚上，野兽都会问她这一天是怎么度过的，然后两人谈论她在宫殿里遇见的许多事情。没过多久，贝蒂就发现野兽那恐吓、凶猛的语气是他笨拙和庞大的体形造成的，并非天性如此。

"这里的一切都合你意吗？"野兽会问。
"好得简直难以置信。"贝蒂会这样回答。

他们聊的时间会长一些。贝蒂向他说起与父亲和哥哥姐姐在家里的生活，野兽聚精会神地听她说，却很少说话。他们的谈话彬彬有礼，可是并不吸引人。野兽只问些简单的问题，通常也只需要贝蒂简短地回答就行了。直到有一次，他突然问："贝蒂，你愿意嫁给我吗？"贝蒂听了差点昏过去。

"Answer yes or no without fear, as it pleases you," he added. Beauty worried that if she said no, in spite of his assurances, it would enrage the Beast or hurt him deeply. But Beauty was honest and courageous.

"No, Beast, I will not," she said plainly after a brief pause. She was afraid of what the Beast might do, but more so, she did not want to insult him after all he had done for her and her father.

"Argh-hhh-hhh!" The Beast sighed so loudly that the dreadful hiss echoed throughout the palace. Beauty sat still in her chair. She didn't know what to expect next. Her answer seemed to have wounded him terribly.

"Then good night to you, Beauty," the Beast said in a disheartened voice as he left the room. He turned to look at her a few times as he walked away.

"Poor Beast," Beauty whispered after a few moments. "How sad that a creature with such a good and generous nature should be so ugly."

"别害怕，你只要回答愿意或不愿意，你怎么想就怎么说。"他又补充了一句。尽管他有言在先，可是贝蒂担心要是自己拒绝，可能会激怒野兽或者深深地伤害他。但是贝蒂为人诚实，又有勇气。

"不，野兽，我不能嫁给你。"经过短暂的沉默后，她坦白地说。她担心野兽会做出什么来，但是她更不想伤害他，毕竟他为父亲和自己付出了这么多。

"啊——啊——啊！"野兽大声叹息，可怕的声音在宫殿里回响。贝蒂仍然坐在椅子上。她不知道接下来会发生什么事。她的回答好像深深地伤害了野兽。

"那么，晚安，贝蒂。"野兽离开房间时与她告别，声音沮丧。他一边走，一边几次回过头来看她。

"可怜的野兽，"过了一会儿，贝蒂轻轻地说，"他这么善良，这么宽宏大量，却长着这么一副可怕的模样，多么可悲啊！"

19

ENCORE

The next day Beauty rose early and continued to explore the palace. As she walked through the grand rooms, she discovered an aviary. It was a mar-velous glass structure filled with hundreds of colorful birds of all sizes and kinds. From talking *parrots* and love birds to *sparrows* and hummingbirds, Beauty found the creatures to be as enchanting as their surroundings.

There were beautiful trees, bushes, shrubs, and birdhouses for them to live in. The birds sang joyful tunes. Beauty welcomed their happy chirping as a pleasant diversion to the hours she spent alone at the palace. In fact, the birds were so friendly that some of them landed on Beauty's hand when she extended it.

"How lovely to hear your pretty song," she said to the little birds that seemed to sing just for her. How nice it would be to have you closer to my chamber, she thought.

In the aviary. Beauty passed a looking glass. In it, she

十九

再次求婚

第二天，贝蒂早早地起床，继续在宫殿里探索。她走过几个大房间，发现了一个大型鸟舍。它是玻璃结构的，里面有数以百计的颜色各异、大小不一的鸟儿。有会说话的鹦鹉，有相思雀，还有麻雀、蜂雀。贝蒂发现这些鸟像周围的环境一样被施了魔法。

那里有漂亮的树木、矮树丛和灌木丛，还有鸟笼供它们住。鸟儿唱着欢快的曲子，贝蒂喜欢它们快乐地唧唧喳喳，为自己独自待在宫殿里的时光消愁解闷。实际上，这些鸟儿非常友好，当贝蒂朝它们伸出手时，有的还停在她手上。

"听你们唱动听的歌曲是多么美妙啊！"她对小鸟们说，似乎它们专为她一人歌唱。她想，要是你们离我的房间近一些那该有多好啊。

在鸟舍里，贝蒂经过一面镜子。在镜子里，她再次看见

113

saw the handsome young man again. This time he extended his hand to her. A small bird was perched on his finger. She peered into the glass and reached out to touch the image, but it disappeared. Again she wondered who the stranger was and whether he needed her help.

Beauty left the aviary and went through another doorway. To her surprise, she was near her own apartment. The aviary and all of its wonderful singing birds were close to her room after all! Somehow, the Beast had provided for her happiness yet again. She was confused by his actions but glad that he seemed to care about her happiness.

Beauty's *curiosity* compelled her to look for the young man. She decided to secretly try to find him while she explored the Beast's castle.

Tired from her long day, Beauty returned to her apartment. She lay down on her bed and drifted off to sleep. In her dream the young man appeared to her. Waking in time to dress for dinner, Beauty sat at the dressing table in her room. Looking in the mirror, she wished to see her father's image again, but it did not appear. She was becoming more concerned for him.

On her way to the dining hall that night, Beauty passed the portrait gallery. Among the pictures was a portrait of a king and beside it one of a queen. The elegant monarchs stared down at Beauty. What a surprise for Beauty when she realized that

那个英俊的小伙子。这次他向她伸出一只手来，一只小鸟停在他的手指上。她盯着镜子看，可是当她伸手去触摸影像时，镜子里的画面消失了。她再次感到好奇，这个陌生人究竟是谁，他是否需要帮助？

贝蒂离开鸟舍，穿过另一扇门。她惊奇地发现自己的房间就在旁边。鸟舍和所有神奇的会歌唱的鸟儿居然就在自己的隔壁！这又是野兽为了让她开心而专门准备的。贝蒂对他的举动感到迷惑不解，不过让她高兴的是，野兽关心着她是否快乐。

好奇心驱使贝蒂寻找镜中的年轻人，她决定在探索城堡时偷偷地找他。

一天下来，贝蒂累坏了。她回到自己的房间，躺倒在床上，渐渐地睡着了。在梦里，那个年轻人又出现了。贝蒂醒来时刚好是吃晚饭的时间，她换上衣服，坐在房里的梳妆台前，想从镜子里再看看父亲，可是父亲的样子并没有出现。她对父亲更是关切了。

那天晚上，在去餐厅的路上，贝蒂经过陈列肖像的长廊。在众多的画像中，有一幅画着一位国王，身边站着王后。这位高贵的君王俯视着贝蒂。贝蒂发现画中的王后跟她在织

the queen in the picture and the woman whose image she had seen in the mirror near the loom were the same person!

What does it all mean? she wondered. Then Beauty heard the horrible sound of the Beast approaching. Since she was still a little frightened of him, she quickly ran to the dining room.

The Beast joined her there and watched her dine just as he had done the night before.

"Beauty, will you marry me?" he asked again when she had finished.

"No, Beast, I cannot," Beauty answered *sincerely*, just as she had answered him the night before.

"Argh-hhh-hhh!" he cried pitifully, leaving the room. Beauty went to her bedchamber troubled by the Beast's deep sadness. She wondered how she could ease his suffering.

"I must find out who that young man is," Beauty whispered. "Perhaps he can tell me why the Beast is so sad and explain all of these puzzles."

Earlier, the magic mirror had shown that her sisters were to be married soon, and her brothers were well employed. Beauty's concern for her family had been eased somewhat, but she was deeply troubled by her father's sadness.

Tired from the day's adventures, and by her own anxieties, Beauty fell into a deep sleep.

布机旁的镜子里看到的妇女竟是同一个人,这多么奇怪啊!

她想知道,这究竟意味着什么? 接着,贝蒂听见了野兽出现时那恐怖的声音。贝蒂对他仍然有些惧怕,所以她赶紧跑到餐厅。

野兽也来到餐厅,就像前一天晚上一样看着贝蒂用餐。

"贝蒂,你愿意嫁给我吗? "等贝蒂吃完饭,野兽再次问她。

"不,野兽,我不能嫁给你。"贝蒂真诚地回答,就跟前一天晚上一样。

"啊——啊——啊! "他令人同情地大叫着离开餐厅。贝蒂回到卧房,被野兽深深的哀伤搅得心神不安。她想知道自己怎么做才能减轻他的痛苦。

"我得找出那个年轻人是谁。"贝蒂轻声说,"或许,他能告诉我为什么野兽如此悲伤,为我揭开所有的谜团。"

早些时候,魔镜曾向她显示她的两个姐姐很快就要结婚了,两个哥哥也找到了好工作。贝蒂对家人的担心减轻了一些,可是父亲的悲伤仍深深地困扰着她。

一天下来,贝蒂身心疲惫,沉沉地睡了过去。

20

TIME PASSES

Day after day. Beauty explored the palace and its grounds. Night after night — always at nine o'clock — the Beast joined her. As Beauty talked, the Beast listened to her stories about when her family lived in the city and how their fortune had changed.

"Yes," the Beast said one night. "Our fates are unpredictable and often can be cruel."

As she spoke during those nighttime visits, it seemed to Beauty that the Beast was sullen and secretive. But she could never get him to speak more openly about himself. She was frustrated and felt sorry for him.

And each night, when the Beast asked her to marry him. Beauty always answered in the same way: "No, Beast, I cannot." Then, without fail, Beauty would hear the pathetic growl with which the Beast soothed his sorrow and signaled his departure for the evening.

二十

时光流逝

日复一日，贝蒂在宫殿及其周围探索着。夜复一夜——总是在九点钟的时候——野兽过来看她。当贝蒂说起她的故事时，野兽总是耐心地听她讲，贝蒂告诉他以前一家人在城里的生活，以及后来他们的命运如何发生了改变。

"是的，"有一天晚上，野兽说，"我们的命运无法预测，而且往往很残酷。"

晚上野兽都来拜访她，贝蒂发现他在听自己说话时，显得闷闷不乐，还遮遮掩掩。贝蒂根本没法让他敞开心怀，多讲讲他自己的事情。对此，她感到沮丧而遗憾。

每天晚上，当野兽向贝蒂求婚时，贝蒂总是说着同样的话："不，野兽，我不能嫁给你。"然后，贝蒂每次都会听见野兽发出悲惨的咆哮声。他以此来缓解内心的痛苦，咆哮之后就预示着他要离开了。

As on the previous evenings, Beauty retired to her room after having rejected the Beast's proposal. As she slept, her mind was filled with images of times past and present. Almost nightly the kind fairy appeared to her in her dreams.

"Beauty, follow your heart," the fairy always advised.

In Beauty's dreams, encounters with the Beast mixed with visions of the handsome young man.

Beauty still had not found out much about the young man, but he was constantly in her dreams and in her thoughts. Now the handsome face of the young man appeared to her more often and at the oddest moments, while she was awake and asleep.

Although Beauty was nearly certain that the Beast meant her no harm, she was afraid to ask him about the young man. Could the Beast be holding him captive, she wondered.

跟以前晚上发生的一样,贝蒂拒绝野兽求婚后回到自己的房间。她睡觉的时候,满脑子想的都是过去和现在的场景,那个和善的精灵几乎夜夜出现在她梦中。

"贝蒂,遵照你内心的想法。"精灵每次都这么忠告。

在贝蒂的梦里,经常交织着出现野兽和那个英俊的小伙子。

贝蒂仍然没有发现关于那个年轻人的线索,可他总是出现在她的梦中和脑海里。现在,贝蒂无论睡着还是醒着,总能更加频繁、不定期地见到这个年轻人的面孔。

尽管贝蒂几乎可以肯定野兽对她没有恶意,可她还是不敢向他打听那个年轻人的事。她怀疑,难道是野兽把他囚禁起来了?

21

SHADOWS IN THE MOONLIGHT

Each day new surprises unfolded to lift Beauty's spirits, but her curiosity about the handsome young man was never satisfied. Perhaps there was no answer to this puzzle, she thought.

One night before retiring. Beauty walked in the rose garden in the moonlight. The arbors were filled with sweet-smelling blossoms of every color. It concerned her that the Beast cared for her so much and that she did not care for him in the same way.

While lost in her thoughts. Beauty came upon a magnificently decorated gazebo with beautiful flowering plants. It stood in the center of the garden. Mirrored panels etched with roses separated each section of the glass walls. When she entered the gazebo, the images on the mirrors startled her. There she was, reflected back in the many mirrors, and by her side was the mysterious young man!

二十一

月光下的阴影

为了让贝蒂振作精神，每天都有新的惊喜呈现在她眼前，可是，她对那个英俊小伙子的好奇心却始终没法得到满足。或许，这是个无法破解的谜团，贝蒂心想。

一天晚上，贝蒂回房之前走进月光下的玫瑰园。凉亭里弥漫着各色玫瑰的芬芳。野兽对她关心有加，可她却没有同样地回报他，这让她很不安。

贝蒂陷入了沉思，不知不觉来到一座华丽的观景台前。观景台就矗立在花园中央，四周开满了鲜花。刻着玫瑰花的镜面将每块玻璃墙分隔开。当她走进观景台，镜子里出现的画面把她吓了一跳。从许多面镜子里映射出她的身影，而她身边居然站着那个神秘的年轻人！

"Who are you?" she asked, determined to find an answer.

"Argh-hhh-hhh!" a cry rang out from a high turret in the castle. Glancing up, Beauty saw the Beast's massive shadow in the window. She was more confused than ever.

The wavering image in the mirror faded. Shaken, Beauty went to her room and finally fell asleep. In her dreams, the fine lady appeared to her again.

"Beauty, follow your heart and you will be rewarded with true happiness," the kind fairy whispered. Then the fairy vanished, and Beauty dreamed of the handsome young man.

"Beauty, don't be swayed by appearances," he begged. Beauty woke with a start. Although the sun had risen, her mind was still clouded.

"你是谁？"她下决心要找到答案。

"啊——啊——啊！"从城堡高处的塔楼上传来一声喊叫。贝蒂循声朝上望去，看见野兽巨大的身影映在窗户上。这让贝蒂更加迷惑不解。

镜子里摇晃不定的影像消失了。贝蒂不住地打战，她回到房间，最后睡了过去。那位仁慈的女士再次出现在她梦中。

"贝蒂，遵照内心的想法，你就会获得真正的快乐。"这位和善的精灵轻声说。接着，精灵消失了，贝蒂又梦见了那个英俊的小伙子。

"贝蒂，不要因为外表而摇摆不定。"他恳求道。贝蒂突然间惊醒。此时太阳已经升起来了，可是贝蒂的脑海里依然疑云密布。

22

THE MAGICAL THEATER

Since the Beast only visited her briefly each evening, Beauty was alone most of the time. Whenever she was lonely, she would think of a diversion and it was magically supplied. One day she found a special room. It was the most amazing marvel yet discovered at the palace, and in it she encountered the most incredible vision of all.

This special room was a *theater*. It was quite dark and had many draped windows. There were many chairs standing vacant, ready for an audience. Golden *candelabra* lined the walls. They lit themselves as she entered. Whenever she sat at one of the chairs, the lights dimmed and the curtain she sat before rolled up. Then she would see a live stage play, an opera or a comedy. Whatever was her wish would appear to her.

Beauty spent much of her time in this room to pass the hours of each day while she waited for dinnertime and the Beast's visit.

二十二

神奇的剧场

野兽只在每天晚上出来见一下贝蒂,其余时间贝蒂都是一个人待着。感到孤独的时候,贝蒂会想到找些乐子解闷,每当这时,她的想法总能神奇地得到满足。有一天,她发现了一个特别的房间。它是贝蒂在宫殿里发现的最令人惊叹的奇观,贝蒂在里面见到的一切简直令人难以置信。

这个特别的房间是一个剧场,里面非常阴暗,窗户上都挂着窗帘。剧场里有许多空位子,是为观众而准备的。墙上有一排金色的枝状大烛台。当贝蒂走进剧场时,它们自动点亮。当她坐到观众席上,灯光又暗了下去,前面的帷幕升了起来。接着,她就可以观赏一出生动的舞台剧、歌剧或是喜剧。她想看什么,台上就演什么。

贝蒂每天都在这个房间花大量时间观赏戏剧,同时等着吃晚饭以及野兽的来访。

One day, a drama unfolded in which the Beast and the handsome young man quarreled over who would be king, and each beckoned Beauty to choose between them! Beauty was so disturbed by the image that she rose from her chair, causing the drama to end abruptly.

Afterward she wished she hadn't acted so *impulsively*. She often returned to the theater to see if that same drama would appear. Perhaps it could give her answers to her many questions, she thought, but it never did.

With so many diversions, time passed quickly, and soon Beauty realized that she had been at the castle for more than three months.

Although he was not witty, the Beast had many fine qualities. Beauty no longer dreaded his visits, but welcomed them. Only two things weighed on her conscience. The first was the Beast's proposals, which he made every night without fail. The second was that although she was very happy at the palace, she still wondered if the handsome young man was being held prisoner by the Beast.

Finally, one night Beauty asked, "Beast, are we alone at the palace?"
"Yes, Beauty, we are alone here," he assured her.

Beauty accepted his answer and finished her meal. Then the Beast proposed to her again.

128

一天，上演了一出戏剧，戏里野兽和那个英俊的小伙子争论谁才是国王，并且请贝蒂从中挑选一个！贝蒂被眼前这一幕搞得心烦意乱，当她从椅子上站起来时，戏剧戛然而止。

之后，她后悔自己当时不该表现得那么冲动。她经常去剧院，想看看那出戏是否还会上演。或许它可以解答她的许多疑惑，贝蒂心想。可是，它再也没上演过。

城堡里有这么多消遣娱乐，所以时间过得特别快。不久，贝蒂发现自己已经在城堡里住了三个多月。

尽管野兽不够机智诙谐，可是他有许多好品质。对他的来访贝蒂不再感到害怕，甚至非常欢迎。只有两件事仍然困扰着她：一是野兽的求婚，每天晚上他都向贝蒂求婚，从不间断；二是尽管她在宫殿里生活得非常快乐，可是仍然想知道那个英俊的小伙子是否被野兽囚禁在城堡里。

最后，有一天晚上，贝蒂问："野兽，宫殿里只有我们两个人吗？"

"是的，贝蒂，只有我们两个。"他向她证实。

贝蒂接受了这个回答，用完了晚餐。接着，野兽又一次向她求婚。

This time, Beauty responded, "I cannot consent to marry you and I cannot deceive you about my heart's intentions. I will always be your friend. Can you be satisfied with that?"

"If I must be satisfied, I will be satisfied. I know I can't expect more. I love you, Beauty, and I can be happy if you stay with me always. Promise that you'll never leave me," he begged.

Beauty felt that she could now make that promise. She was quite happy with the Beast at the palace. He saw to her every need, and it was due to his generosity that her family once again prospered. All but one of her desires were met there. Beauty longed to see her father again. Lately, whenever she peered into the mirror in her room, she could see that he was unhappy. "If he knew that I am well and content, he would be happy again," she *murmured*.

这次，贝蒂回答说："我不同意嫁给你，我不能违背自己的心意欺骗你。我永远都是你的朋友，这样的关系能让你感到满意吗？"

"如果只有这样的选择，我会满足的，我知道不能有更多奢望。我爱你，贝蒂，如果你能一直待在我身边，我会快乐的。答应我，你永远都不会离开我。"他乞求道。

贝蒂觉得现在她可以做出这个承诺。她在宫殿里与野兽生活得非常快乐，野兽能看透她想要的一切，而且因为他的慷慨，贝蒂家又富了起来。贝蒂还有唯一一个心愿没有实现，她渴望再次见到父亲。近来，只要她往房间的镜子里看，总会见到父亲闷闷不乐的神情。"要是他知道我一切安好，那他就会重新开心起来。"贝蒂喃喃自语。

23

BEAUTY'S REQUEST

"Beast," Beauty said, "I will promise never to leave you, but I must see my father again. He needs me. I will die of worry if I can't see him again."

"I Would rather die myself than cause you harm,"the Beast sighed.

"Will you allow me to go to him then?"she asked.

"I will send you to your father, Beauty. You can stay with him, and in so doing I will die of grief for losing you," he wailed.

Beauty looked tenderly at the Beast. "Beast, I promise to return in one week if you permit me to go. You have already shown me through the mirror that my sisters are married and that my brothers have gone into the king's service. Just let me spend a week with my dear father. He is all alone and not well. I will willingly return to you then," Beauty pleaded. "It has been so long since I have seen him, and he needs me."

"Do you promise to return after one week?" the Beast asked.

二十三
贝蒂的请求

"野兽，"贝蒂说，"我答应永远都不离开你，可是我必须去见见我的父亲，他需要我。要是我没法见到他，我会忧虑而死的。"

"我宁愿自己死掉也不想给你带来伤害。"野兽叹了口气，说。

"那么你允许我去见见他吗？"她问。

"贝蒂，我会把你送去你父亲那儿。你可以跟他待在一起，不过这么一来，我会因为失去你伤心过度而死。"他悲叹。

贝蒂温柔地看着野兽。"野兽，如果你允许我回去，我答应你只要一个星期就回来。你已经通过镜子让我看到两个姐姐已经嫁人，两个哥哥也进宫为国王效力，就让我跟亲爱的父亲一起住一个星期吧。他一个人十分孤单，而且也不快乐。一个星期后我会心甘情愿地回到你身边。"贝蒂恳求他，"我已经很久没有见到他了，他需要我。"

"你保证一星期后会回来？"野兽问。

Beauty was alarmed by the desperate look in his eyes. "Yes," she answered sincerely.

"Then you can go. You will be there in the morning," the Beast said. "When you are ready to return, turn your ring around on your finger before going to sleep and say, 'I wish to return to my Beast.' Farewell, Beauty," he said. His sigh rattled the walls.

That night Beauty was very distressed for having caused the Beast to grieve so deeply. She also dreamed again of the handsome young man.

"Beauty how can you abandon me?" he asked.

Beauty awoke abruptly.

Troubled by the dream, and concerned about the Beast, Beauty knew what she had to do. She was determined to make her visit and return as soon as she was sure of her father's well-being.

After that, she slept peacefully, trusting that all would be well.

看到野兽流露出绝望的眼神，贝蒂感到惶恐不安。"是的。"她真诚地回答。

"那么你可以走。明天早上就到家了。"野兽说，"当你准备回来的时候，只要在临睡前转动你手上的戒指，一边说'我想回到我的野兽身边'就可以了。再见，贝蒂。"他的叹息声使得周围的墙壁咯吱作响。

那天晚上，贝蒂十分难过，因为自己让野兽这么痛苦。她又一次梦见了那个英俊的小伙子。

"贝蒂，你怎么可以抛弃我？"他问。

贝蒂一下子惊醒了。

受这个梦困扰，又担心着野兽，贝蒂清楚这时自己该怎么做。她决定回去后，一旦确信父亲过得幸福安宁，她就赶紧回来。

之后，她平静地睡了过去——相信一切都会好起来的。

24

A FAMILY REUNION

Beauty woke late the next morning. As the sun streamed through a small circular window, she looked around, a bit bewildered, before recognizing that now she was in her loft room at her father's cottage in the country. Silently, she thanked the Beast.

How good is my Beast that he has seen to my happiness yet again and made this wish above all others come true! she marveled.

The room was now finely furnished, and the country house had been repaired due to the treasure her father had gotten from the Beast. Beauty rang the little bell that was on the bedside table. A maid entered and nearly fainted at seeing her standing in a robe and slippers in the middle of the room.

"What is it, Jeannette?" asked the merchant running up to the loft to see what had happened.

二十四
合家团圆

　　第二天早上，贝蒂很晚才醒来。当阳光射进圆形小窗户时，她环顾四周，感到有点儿迷惑，后来才意识到她回到了父亲乡下的农舍，正在自己那间阁楼里。她默默地感谢野兽。

　　我的野兽多好啊！他又一次满足了我的快乐，帮助我实现了这个最大的愿望。对此，她大为惊奇。

　　房间现在布置得很好，农舍也经过了一番整修。这都得益于父亲从野兽那里得到的财富。贝蒂按响了床头柜上的小铃。女仆走进阁楼，见到贝蒂穿着睡衣和拖鞋站在房中央，差点吓晕过去。

　　"珍妮特，怎么回事？"商人问。他跑上阁楼，想看看发生了什么事。

"Beauty, you have returned!" he exclaimed, hugging his daughter. "But how — ?"

"The Beast allowed it, but I must return to the palace in one week, Father," Beauty said. "I promised him that I would return to him. He is so good to me," she said.

"Yes, when it is time, but for now let me look at you!" rejoiced her father.

So happy were father and daughter in their reunion that they smiled and hugged each other for a long time. Then the merchant told Beauty how, with the riches sent by the Beast, he was able to become a prosperous merchant again. Beauty told him of the good times she had experienced at the Beast's palace.

"Father, there is such enchantment there. More than you can imagine," Beauty continued, telling him about the marvels she discovered there and about the handsome young man.

"I do not know what it all means," the merchant said. "Perhaps there is no answer, only your imagination conjuring the image, and he is not a prisoner of the palace but a prisoner of your dreams," he proposed.

"I wonder too, Father," she said thoughtfully.

"Sir, there is a trunk in the next room," the maid declared, interrupting their *reunion*. A trunk filled with gowns embellished with gold, diamonds, and jewels of every type was in the next room. Beauty thanked the Beast again for this sign of his affection for her. She chose a gown to wear and put aside the remaining dresses for her sisters.

"贝蒂,你回来啦!"他大叫起来,拥抱自己的女儿,"可是,你怎么——"

"父亲,是野兽准许我回来的,不过,一个星期以后我必须回宫殿去。"贝蒂说,"我答应他我会回到他身边。他对我太好了。"她说。

"好,到时候再说,现在让我看看你!"她父亲高兴地说。

对于这次团聚,父女俩都十分开心,他们又是欢笑,又是拥抱,就这样过了好长时间。接着,商人告诉贝蒂,野兽给他的财富让他再次成为富商。贝蒂告诉他自己在野兽的宫殿里度过的美好时光。

"父亲,那真是个充满魔法的地方。远比你想象的还要多。"贝蒂接着告诉父亲她在那里发现的奇观,还有那个英俊的年轻人。

"我不知道这意味着什么,"商人说,"或许根本没有答案,只是你的幻觉,他并没有囚禁在宫殿里,而是禁锢在你梦中。"他提出自己的看法。

"父亲,我也怀疑是这样的。"她若有所思。

"先生,隔壁房间里有一口大箱子。"女仆打断了他们。箱子里全是各式各样缀满金银珠宝的衣服,就在隔壁房间里。贝蒂再次感谢野兽对她的关爱。她挑了一件衣服穿上,把其余的全都留给姐姐。

"Elise and Rene will look lovely in these," she said to her father. As she said these words, the trunk and gowns disappeared!

"Beauty, it seems that the Beast wants you to keep these for yourself," her father said. Then the gowns and the trunk reappeared.

"You must be right. Father," Beauty agreed, laughing gaily at this latest enchantment.

While Beauty dressed, her father spread the news of her return. When the horse-drawn coaches carrying her sisters and their husbands arrived, Beauty went downstairs to the parlor to greet them.

Soon Beauty's whole family surrounded her. Her brothers were there on leave from the king's service for a short time. They joyously gave her great bear hugs, while her sisters expressed their astonishment.

"We thought you were lost for sure," Elise said. "How happy we are that you have returned to us." Her eyes were fixed on the jeweled choker around Beauty's neck.

Rene nodded her head, admiring the lovely gown that Beauty wore.

The gown was made of the most extraordinary silk and satin materials. Pearls were embroidered along the neckline.

"伊莉斯和雷内穿上这些衣服肯定很漂亮。"她对父亲说。就在她说话的时候,箱子和所有的衣服一下子不见了!

"贝蒂,看样子野兽只想把这些衣服给你一个人。"她父亲说。接着,衣服和箱子又出现了。

"一定是被你说中了,父亲。"贝蒂同意他的话,对眼前的魔法开心地笑了起来。

当贝蒂换衣服的时候,父亲把她回来的消息传了出去。当马车载着她的两个姐姐和她们的丈夫来到农舍时,贝蒂下楼到客厅迎接他们。

不一会儿,贝蒂的家人全都围在她身边。她的两个哥哥请了短假从国王身边回来看她。他们满心欢喜地紧紧拥抱贝蒂,但她那两个姐姐对她的归来表示惊讶。

"我们还以为你肯定没有了呢,"伊莉斯说,"你能回到我们中间,我们有多么高兴啊。"她的眼睛盯着贝蒂脖子上的宝石项链。

雷内点着头,她正羡慕贝蒂身上的漂亮衣服。

这身衣服是用最奇特的绸缎制成的,领口镶嵌着珍珠。

The dress had a short train so that Beauty looked like a *princess* wearing it. In truth, it was the most simple of the gowns in the trunk, but it was the perfect complement to Beauty's natural loveliness.

Beauty welcomed her sisters and their husbands with open arms and hugs of genuine affection. Her own happiness was obvious and her love for her sisters unconditional. Elise and Rene were more jealous than ever of Beauty.

Elise whispered to Rene, "She seems so happy."

"And here we are," Rene whispered back, "stuck with miserable husbands."

"It isn't fair," they said in unison.

Elise had married a man who was very good looking but so conceited that he cared only about his own needs and desires. Rene had married a very clever man, but he was stingy and *mean*. His constant criticisms tortured Rene, and they quarreled all of the time.

Now their husbands were fawning over Beauty!

Beauty told everyone about the magical palace and the generous Beast.

She assured them that she was happy. The Beast saw to her every need. She told them that her promise to return was

裙摆很短，这让贝蒂看上去像个公主。其实，这不过是箱子里最平常的一件衣服，但却最能衬托出贝蒂的可爱。

贝蒂张开双臂欢迎她的姐姐和姐夫，真诚地拥抱他们。她的快乐显而易见，她无条件地爱着两位姐姐。伊莉斯和雷内比以前更加嫉妒贝蒂了。

伊莉斯轻声地对雷内说："她看上去多快活。"
"而我们，"雷内小声说，"却被糟糕的丈夫牵绊住。"

"这不公平。"她们齐声说。

伊莉斯嫁给了一个外表好看却自以为是的人，他只关心自己的需求和欲望。雷内嫁给了一个聪明人，可是他吝啬又卑劣。他经常指责雷内，让她饱受折磨，两人为此总是吵个不停。

现在她们的丈夫正在讨好贝蒂！

贝蒂向他们讲述了那座不可思议的城堡和慷慨大方的野兽。

她让家人相信，她在那儿过得很开心，野兽满足了她的一切需求。她说自己是真心实意地答应野兽会回去，而不仅

truly her wish and not just in gratitude for all the Beast had done for her and her family.

Elise and Rene were enraged by Beauty's good fortune and were determined to make her miserable.

是感激野兽为她和她的家人所做的一切。

　　伊莉斯和雷内被贝蒂的好运激怒了，她们决定让她吃苦头。

25

ENVY EVERLASTING

Elise and Rene left the parlor to take a breath of fresh air alone in the garden.

"How unimaginable it is to me that our wretched little sister should be so happy!" Rene complained as she wiped a tear from her eyes.

"How can she be the one to look so beautiful and content after all we've been through?" Elise hissed through clenched teeth. "We must not let her return to the Beast."

"Yes, Elise. Then the Beast will become so angry that he'll devour her for breaking her word," Rene conspired.

Elise and Rene pretended to be crushed by the thought of Beauty leaving the family again.

"Oh, dear sister," Rene pleaded, "you must stay with us. Father needs you. Without you, he will die."

"Beauty, it is our dream come true that our little sister has returned home and is safe. Stay with us," Elise added.

二十五

无休止的嫉妒

伊莉斯和雷内撇开家人，离开客厅，到花园里呼吸新鲜空气。

"真是难以想象啊，我们可怜的小妹妹竟然可以这么快活！"雷内抱怨着，擦去了一滴眼泪。

"我们经历了那么多苦难，她怎么还可以一个人看上去这么漂亮、这么得意呢？"伊莉斯从牙缝里蹦出这些话，"我们一定不能让她回到野兽那里。"

"是的，伊莉斯。那样的话，野兽会因为她食言而大发雷霆，把她吞掉。"雷内与她密谋。

伊莉斯和雷内假装一想到贝蒂再次离家就伤心欲绝。

"哦，亲爱的妹妹，"雷内恳求说，"你一定得待在我们身边。父亲需要你，没有你，他会死的。"

"贝蒂，我们的梦想成真了，我们的小妹妹安全回家了。留在我们身边吧。"伊莉斯接着说。

Elise and Rene were so kind to their younger sister that Beauty was overjoyed at their change of heart. They made such a fuss over the prospect of her leaving them that they cried uncontrollably and tore at their hair.

"Father will simply die if you leave again," Elise said.
"Yes," Rene agreed, "his heart will surely break."

Torn between causing the Beast's death and her father's. Beauty did not know what to do. She was tormented, but hoped that if she stayed home a little while longer, she could convince her family that she would be safe at the palace.

伊莉斯和雷内对妹妹如此友善，她们的转变让贝蒂大喜过望。想到贝蒂再次离家，她俩大惊小怪的，哭得难以自禁，还撕扯自己的头发。

"要是你再次离开，父亲一定会死的。"伊莉斯说。
"是啊，"雷内附和说，"他的心都会碎了。"

一边是野兽会死掉，一边是父亲活不了，贝蒂夹在中间不知如何是好。她内心承受着煎熬，心里想的是在家里多住一小会儿，趁这个时间说服家人，她在宫殿里会平平安安的。

26

THE DREAM

Many nights after the week's deadline had past, Beauty dreamed that she was in the palace rose garden. The Beast was lying on the grass near a *pond*. His breathing was strained and he seemed to be in pain. He whispered, "Beauty, why have you not returned to me?"

The dream faded, and another one took its place. In this dream, the kind fairy appeared to her. "Beauty, you have broken your promise. The Beast is dying," the fairy said *sadly*.

"No!" Beauty called out, waking from the dream with a start. She sat up and began to cry. At that moment, she realized that she loved the Beast. The vision of the handsome young man was probably nothing more than that — a fleeting image. The Beast had said that they were alone, so perhaps her father was right. After all, during her stay with her family Beauty had not dreamed of the young man at all.

How wicked of me to break my promise to my Beast, she

二十六

梦　境

一个星期的期限早已过去，许多天之后的一个夜晚，贝蒂梦见自己身在宫殿的玫瑰园里，野兽躺在池塘边的草地上，呼吸急促，好像十分痛苦。他声音微弱："贝蒂，为什么你还不回到我身边？"

这个梦消失后，又出现了另外一个梦，那位和善的精灵出现在梦中。"贝蒂，你食言了。野兽快要死了。"精灵悲伤地说。

"不要！"贝蒂大喊一声，从梦中惊醒。她坐起身，哭了起来。在那一刻，她意识到自己爱上了野兽。印象中的英俊小伙子或许不过是短暂的幻影，野兽说过城堡里只有他们两人，可能父亲说对了。毕竟，与家人住在一起的时间里，贝蒂从来没有梦见过那个年轻人。

我多么恶劣啊，居然违背了对野兽许下的诺言，贝蒂心

thought. He was so kind and thoughtful. I should not have refused to marry him. I know now that I would be happy with him. I could never forgive myself if he suffered or died because of me.

She turned the ring on her finger and said, "I want to return to my Beast."

Beauty fell back to sleep, and when she woke she was at the Beast's palace.

想。他是那么友善、体贴，我真不应该拒绝嫁给他。现在我知道跟他在一起会让我快乐。要是他因为我而受苦甚至死去，我永远都不能原谅自己。

她转动手上的戒指，说："我想要回到我的野兽身边。"

贝蒂又睡了过去，等她醒来时，已经在野兽的宫殿里了。

27

SEARCHING FOR THE BEAST

"I am back!" Beauty cried out with joy when she saw that she was at the palace. She dressed in a hurry and went to look for the Beast. It was early morning. She couldn't find him anywhere. Since he never walked about the palace during the day, she thought, he'll come in the evening while I dine, as he always does.

Beauty spent the day in her usual activities but anxiously awaited the Beast's arrival at nine o'clock. The hours at the palace never passed so slowly as they did that day.

She went into the aviary to enjoy the birds' happy songs, but their *melodies* were sad.

She went into the music room to play the harp, but the tune was *melancholy* and did not entertain her.

二十七

寻找野兽

"我回来啦！"当贝蒂发现自己回到宫殿时，快乐地大叫起来。她急忙穿好衣服，出去寻找野兽。现在是大清早，她到处找都找不到。野兽白天从来不在宫殿里走动，她想，等到吃晚饭的时候他就会出现，他总是这样的。

贝蒂跟平常一样消磨白天，可是心里焦急地等待着晚上九点野兽的到来。那天宫殿里的时间比以前任何时候过得都要慢。

她来到鸟舍聆听鸟儿快乐的歌唱，可是，它们的旋律听起来是悲伤的。

她来到音乐室弹奏竖琴，可是，忧伤的曲调没法让她高兴起来。

She went to the library to read a favorite book, but couldn't concentrate on the story.

She went to the theater room, which always lifted her spirits, but this time the show did not interest her.

At the gazebo Beauty found that even the flowers seemed *wilted*.

Finally, it was time for dinner. Beauty dressed in one of the best gowns she could find and went to the banquet hall. The clock struck nine, but the Beast did not come to talk with her.

"Oh, where is my Beast?" Beauty wailed, giving in to the emotions that had clouded her mind and heart throughout the long and wearying day.

Beauty's dream flashed through her mind. She was afraid that the Beast was dead. She ran from room to room in the palace, searching for him. "Beast, Beast, where are you?" she called out. Worrying about the Beast consumed her every thought.

Wringing her hands in despair, her hopes ever sinking, Beauty recalled that in her dream she had seen the Beast lying on the grass near a pond in the garden. She ran there as quickly as she could.

　　她来到图书室阅读喜爱的书籍，可是却不能集中精神。

　　她又来到剧场，那儿总能让她精神振奋，可是，这次的演出却吸引不了她。

　　在观景台，她发现就连花儿好像都枯萎了。

　　最后，晚餐时间到了。贝蒂从她能找到的最好的衣服中挑了一件换上，然后来到宴会厅。时钟敲过九下，可是，野兽并没有出来跟她说话。

　　"哦，我的野兽在哪里啊？"贝蒂号啕大哭，尽情发泄。在这漫长而又疲惫的一天，她的心头始终笼罩着一层乌云。

　　贝蒂的梦闪现在她脑海里，她担心野兽已经死了。她从宫殿这个房间跑到那个房间，寻找野兽。"野兽，野兽，你在哪里？"她大声呼唤，心里面全是对野兽的担忧。

　　就在她绝望地绞着双手，希望渐渐破灭的时候，贝蒂回想起梦中她见到野兽躺在花园里池塘边的草地上。她以最快的速度朝那个地方跑去。

There he was, his huge body sprawled on the ground. His breath Was short and choked. He was barely conscious when she bent down to feel his *pulse*. Even though his pulse was weak, she could feel the faint beating of his heart. She drew water from the pond and gently splashed his face with it.

"You broke your promise," the Beast whispered.

"My poor Beast," Beauty cried, tenderly holding his hand in hers.

"When you didn't return, I could not eat or sleep," the Beast moaned.

"Beast, you must not die!" Beauty said. "I cannot live without you. I love you. Beast. I will marry you!"

Gently, Beauty kissed his cheek. Brilliant lights and fireworks went off above the palace. *Cannons* blasted into the air, and music swelled around them.

The statues in the courtyard and throughout the palace suddenly came to life. A golden chariot drawn by a unicorn emerged from the mist that surrounded the palace. Beauty hardly noticed any of this. Her only concern was for the Beast's well-being.

野兽就在那儿，他巨大的身子平躺在地上，呼吸急促。当贝蒂俯身触摸他的脉搏时，他几乎没有了意识。尽管他脉搏微弱，可是贝蒂能够感觉到他的心在微弱地跳动。她从池塘里取了些水，轻轻地洒到他脸上。

"你食言了。"野兽轻声说。

"我可怜的野兽。"贝蒂哭了起来，温柔地握住他的手。

"在你没回来的日子里，我吃不下饭，睡不着觉。"野兽呻吟着。

"野兽，你不准死！"贝蒂说，"没有你我也活不下去。我爱你，野兽。我要嫁给你！"

贝蒂轻轻地吻了吻野兽的脸颊。这时，宫殿上空出现了璀璨的灯光和焰火。礼炮在空中鸣响，音乐在四周弥漫。

院子以及整个宫殿里的雕像突然之间全都活了过来，一头独角兽驾着一辆金色的战车从弥漫在宫殿四周的薄雾中出现。贝蒂几乎没有注意到周围的任何变化，她唯一关心的是野兽的安康。

28

NO LONGER A BEAST

Wiping the tears from her eyes, Beauty looked at the Beast. But the Beast was gone! In his place was the handsome young man!

"Who are you?" Beauty asked. "And where is my Beast?"

"Beauty, I am the Beast. Your love has broken the spell under which I have lived for years, alone and in pain. Your friendship and companionship restored my hope that I would rule here as a prince, and no longer as a Beast. But when you left, all of my hopes died. I wanted to die, too."

The sound of the unicorn drew their attention to the chariot that had appeared in the garden. Two women stepped from it. Both were dressed in fine clothing. Beauty recognized one as the kind fairy in her dreams. The other woman wore a crown and a royal robe. Beauty recognized her from the portrait in the gallery.

"Well, Your Majesty," the fairy said as she and the queen

二十八

野兽变身

贝蒂擦干眼泪，看着野兽。可是野兽却不见了，取而代之的是那个英俊的小伙子！

"你是谁？"贝蒂问，"我的野兽去哪儿啦？"

"贝蒂，我就是野兽。是你的爱解除了施加在我身上的符咒——因为它，这些年来我一直生活在孤独和痛苦中。你的友谊和陪伴重新点燃了我作为王子而不是野兽来统治这个地方的希望。可是，当你离开时，我万念俱灰，甚至想一死了之。"

独角兽的声音让他们注意到了那辆战车。它就在花园里。从车上走下来两位衣着华丽的妇人，贝蒂认出其中一个就是出现在她梦里的那位和善的精灵；另一个妇人头戴王冠，身披皇袍，贝蒂认出她就是走廊上那幅画像里的女人。

精灵和女王向这对快乐的年轻人走来，精灵说："陛下，

approached the happy young couple, "here is Beauty, the only young woman who could break the spell that doomed your son to live in the form of a beast. You will never find a more loving, caring, and devoted daughter-in-law."

Beauty curtsied before the queen, who stepped forward and took Beauty's hands in both of hers.

"Thank you, Beauty, for all you have done to restore my son and his kingdom," the queen exclaimed.

Then the queen placed her arms around the prince and hugged him with such happiness and joy that, once again, fireworks and cannons went off around the palace. The people who had been statues danced merrily.

"You see, Beauty," said the kind fairy, "all that exists here was created to protect the prince until he could be restored to his human form."

Beauty was amazed and thrilled to discover that her Beast and the handsome young man were one and the same being.

"Beauty, because of the enchantment I was not able to reveal my identity to you. I could only let you see my true self in the reflections cast by mirrors and in your dreams."

"Those images confused me and nearly led my heart astray," Beauty said lovingly. "How long have you suffered?" she asked the prince.

这就是贝蒂——唯一能解除让你儿子变成野兽的符咒的小姐。你再也找不到比她更钟情、更有爱心、更甘于奉献的媳妇了。"

贝蒂朝女王屈膝行礼，女王走上前用双手握住贝蒂的手。

"谢谢你，贝蒂，感谢你为我儿和他的王国所做的一切。"女王说。

接着，女王把手臂搭在王子身上，快乐地拥抱他。这时，焰火再次出现在宫殿上空，礼炮声又一次在周围响起。那些由雕像变回来的人快乐地跳起舞来。

"你瞧，贝蒂，"和善的精灵说，"这里的一切都是为了保护王子而存在，直到他恢复人形。"

贝蒂大吃一惊，激动地发现她的野兽和这个英俊的年轻人竟然是同一个人。

"贝蒂，因为受魔法控制，所以我没法向你表明自己的身份，我只能让你在镜子里和梦境中看见我真实的形象。"

"这些形象困扰着我，差点让我的心陷入迷途。"贝蒂怜爱地说，"你受魔法控制多长时间了？"她问王子。

"I can hardly remember now how long it has been," the prince said. He took Beauty's hand as they sat in the rose garden. "It seems like forever. Before you came, I had no hope."

"我现在也记不清到底有多久了。"他们坐在玫瑰园里，王子握住贝蒂的手向她诉说，"似乎没有尽头。在你到来以前，我看不到任何希望。"

29

THE EVIL FAIRY

"My story begins when an evil fairy sought to increase her power and control my destiny. It was this fairy who caused my *transformation* from man to Beast."

"In my youth the *alliance* between mortals and fairies was strong," the prince explained. "The murals in the great hall depict a time when fairies and kings were allies who helped one another against invading armies, *imps*, ogres, witches and sorcerers."

Beauty remembered the murals that had captivated her when she first arrived at the palace.

"Each envied the other's power, though," the kind fairy said. "Some fairies believed our mystical abilities outweighed worldly matters and made us superior to men, and the king — the most sovereign ruler of all the land, who answered to no one but the divine — would never concede to such a thing."

Beauty listened to the incredible tale. Could this be true? she thought.

166

二十九

邪恶的精灵

"我的故事开始于一个邪恶的精灵想要扩张她的权力、控制我的命运,正是这个精灵把我从人变成了野兽。"

"我小时候,人类和精灵的联盟是坚固的。"王子解释说,"大厅的壁画上描绘了那个时期精灵和国王结成同盟,互相帮助,对抗入侵的敌人——妖魔、鬼怪和男女巫师。"

贝蒂记起,她第一次来到宫殿就被那些壁画所吸引。

"尽管双方都嫉妒对方的力量,"和善的精灵说,"可是,有些精灵相信我们神秘的能力超越了世间的一切,使我们比人类更优越,而国王——这片土地至高无上的统治者,只听从神灵的指示——对此却从来没有让步。"

贝蒂听着这个令人难以置信的故事。难道这会是真的?她心想。

"One such powerful fairy was a confidante to my father, the king. She was both feared and loved," the prince said.

"Mostly feared," the queen added, "since she was unpredictable and was known to take offense easily — often taking merciless vengeance on the offender."

"When my father died, this fairy helped my mother raise me. Wise men of the court advised it so as not to anger the fairy. She was charged with my education and keeping me safe from harm. This she did, but in so doing her own ambitions and desire for control overcame her. In my father's untimely death, which elevated me as his heir to the kingdom, she saw her opportunity."

"Yes," the queen said, taking her son's arm affectionately. "She cared for the prince while I was defending his kingdom against a neighboring army."

"As I grew older and wanted to assist my mother in the campaign to protect my kingdom," the prince continued, "the fairy refused to let me join my mother on the battlefield. When, at last, my mother returned in triumph years later, the fairy approached her with the plan she had devised ever since my father's death."

The prince, the queen, and the kind fairy recalled the events that led to that horrible, fateful day when all the prince-turned-beast could do was wait... and wait....

"有一个力量强大的精灵是我父王的知己，她让人又爱又怕。"王子说。

"非常地害怕，"女王补充说，"因为她不可捉摸，而且报复心极强，经常残忍地报复那些得罪过她的人。"

"父王去世以后，这位精灵帮助母后抚养我，朝中有些睿智的大臣建议不要去惹她。她负责我的学习、保护我的安全。这些她确实做到了，可是在这个过程中，她的野心和控制欲不断膨胀。我父亲死得突然，于是，我成了他的王国的继承人。这时，她认为她的机会来了。"

"是的，"王后慈爱地挽起儿子的手臂，"当我与入侵的邻国军队作战、保卫这个国家时，她代为照料王子。"

"当我渐渐长大，想要协助母后作战、保卫我的王国时，精灵拒绝我上战场帮助母后。"王子接着说，"自从我父王去世，她就一直在密谋，等到多年以后母后终于凯旋归来，她才开始实施自己的计划。"

王子、王后、和善的精灵一起回想往事——在那段在劫难逃的可怕的日子里，变成野兽的王子只能守候……不断守候……

30

RELIVING THE PAST

"Good Queen, welcome home. Here is your son," said the evil fairy, presenting the prince.

The queen had not been to the palace in quite a while. It had been the king's summer *retreat*. The queen chose it for her homecoming after the war to rest and regain her strength and peace of mind.

"Thank you for all you have done to keep my son safe," the queen said. "How can I ever repay you?"

The question, so innocently asked, was what the evil fairy wanted to hear.

"My Queen, now that you have returned and your son's kingdom is secure, I demand that you let us marry. I will be his wife, and as a queen with magical powers, I will protect his safety and prosperity," she stated boldly.

Without a moment's *hesitation*, the queen cried, "Are you mad?"

三十

往日再现

"我的好女王，欢迎您归来。我把您的儿子交还给您。"说着，邪恶的精灵把王子带了出来。

女王已经很久没有回宫了,这里过去是国王夏季避暑的地方。战争结束了，女王凯旋归来，她选择来这里休养，恢复体力，并且让内心宁静下来。

"感谢你为保护我儿所做的一切，"女王说，"我该怎么回报你呢？"

问者无心，可是邪恶的精灵等的就是这句话。

"我的女王，既然您已经回来，您儿子的王国也安全了，我要求你让我们俩结婚。我将成为他的妻子，身为一个拥有魔法的女王，我会保护他的安全和王国的繁荣。"她明目张胆地提出要求。

女王立刻叫了起来："你疯了吗？"

The prince, too, thought the fairy's demand was an unbelievable one. He wanted to marry someone of his own choosing and someone he loved.

"Why is it absurd, madam?" the fairy questioned. "There would be no more powerful kingdom on earth than your son's if he were to marry me."

The queen merely raised her head and, looking by chance into the great mirror, said, "Can you not see for yourself why?" she asked.

The prince's gentle reflection stood in sharp contrast to the hard, spiteful countenance of the fairy, whose rage was growing.

"I lower myself to marry a mere mortal, when I could choose from the most powerful genies in the universe," she cried. "You should be honored at my proposal! What do you say, young prince? Do you refuse to marry me?"

"Yes, I refuse to marry you," he answered. "We can repay you some other way."

"*Insignificant* vain mortals! You shall pay for your *insolence*!" she said, striking the prince.

Overcome by the shock of the blow, the prince fell to the ground. He tried to rise but couldn't. He was so heavy, he could only lift himself a few inches from the ground. His hands were now huge paws. His body had been transformed into that of a massive beast!

王子也认为精灵的要求不可思议。他想娶一个自己挑选的、为自己所爱的女子为妻。

"难道这很荒谬吗，夫人？"精灵质问道，"如果你儿子跟我结婚，那么世上再也不会有比他的王国更强大的国家了。"

女王抬起头，无意中看见一面大镜子。"难道你自己还不明白吗？"她只是问了这样一句。

镜中的王子温文尔雅，与之形成鲜明对照的是，愤怒不断膨胀的精灵，面容冷酷而恶毒。

"我原可以从全世界最强大的神灵中挑选夫君，可是我却屈尊嫁给一个凡人。"她叫嚷着，"你应该为我向你儿子求婚感到荣耀！小王子，你怎么说？难道你也不肯娶我吗？"

"是的，我拒绝娶你为妻，"他回答，"我们可以用别的方式报答你。"

"渺小而又自负的人类啊！你们要为自己的傲慢付出代价！"她一边说着，一边殴打王子。

王子被这突如其来的一击打倒在地。他试着站起来，可是做不到，他觉得身子很沉，只能把自己撑离地面几英寸。此时，他的双手变成了巨大的爪子，身体变成了庞大的野兽。

"Now find someone more to your liking!" the evil fairy laughed. "Without your title, without your good looks, without your wit or charm, see if you can find someone to love you. Until you do, you will remain in the *hideous* form of a dim-witted beast. And should you dare to tell anyone what has happened here, you will be doomed forevermore!" Then she disappeared.

The prince-turned-beast and his mother were devastated, until a gentle voice reassuringly called out: "Take courage! It will take time, but hope and love can change one's destiny."

Fortunately, the kind fairy was in the great hall at the time.

"Can you help us?" the queen asked.

"Perhaps," the fairy answered. "By meeting the condition of the spell it could be broken. I will find a girl whose heart is true," she promised.

"What about the people who have seen the transformation?" the queen asked with concern.

"I will cast a spell over everyone at the palace to keep them frozen in time until the evil spell is broken."

The prince and the queen agreed.

"But you must be careful," she cautioned the prince. "Keep your secret. Your power of speech will be your undoing if you reveal what has happened to you. That is why the wicked fairy changed only your form, and not your abilities."

　　"现在去找更合你胃口的人吧！"邪恶的精灵笑了起来，"没有了王子的头衔，没有了光鲜的外表，没有了智慧与魅力，看你还能不能找到爱你的人。除非你找到这样的人，否则你永远是丑陋愚笨的野兽。要是你胆敢向任何人提及这里发生的事，那么你永远都恢复不了人形。"说完她就消失了。

　　变成野兽的王子和他的母后陷入了绝望，直到有一个温柔的声音响起："振作起来！这需要时间，不过希望和爱可以改变一个人的命运。"

　　幸运的是，这个和善的精灵当时正在大厅里。

　　"你能帮助我们吗？"女王问。
　　"或许可以，"精灵回答，"遇见爱你的人后，这个符咒就会解开。我会找到一个真心实意的姑娘。"她许下诺言。

　　"那些看见我儿变身的人怎么办？"女王关切地问。

　　"我会给宫殿里每个人身上施加咒语，把他们冻结起来，直到邪恶的符咒解开。"

　　王子和王后同意了。

　　"不过你自己务必当心，"她提醒王子，"保守你的秘密。因为你还能说话，要是把发生在你身上的事情泄露出去，就真的会毁于一旦。这就是为什么邪恶的精灵只是改变你的外形，却保留了你的技能的原因。"

Then the kind fairy waved her wand and said a few magic words. Everyone at the summer palace except the queen, the Beast, and the kind fairy, turned to stone, and a heavy mist rose up around the estate to keep passersby away.

The Beast kept himself secluded at the palace. Occasionally, the fairy visited the Beast to let him know of her progress in finding a solution.

The weeks turned into months, then years. His one comfort was seeing the many wonders at the palace. He especially loved the rose garden that he cultivated. It was these beloved roses that had finally brought Beauty to him.

It seemed that the Beast's waiting was over when the merchant became lost in the woods. When he heard about the merchant's kind-hearted daughter, the Beast began to hope once again. And then the good fairy's plan began to unfold...

接着，和善的精灵挥动手里的魔杖，念了几句咒语。于是，夏宫里所有的人，除了王后、野兽和精灵本人，都变成了石头，宫殿附近升起一股浓雾，防止路人靠近。

野兽在宫殿里与世隔绝。偶尔，精灵会来拜访野兽，告诉他找人的进展。

时间一周一周、一月一月，甚至一年一年地过去了，他唯一的安慰就是能够见到宫殿里许多奇观。他尤其喜欢亲自栽培的玫瑰园，正是这些可爱的玫瑰最终把贝蒂带到了他身边。

当商人迷失在森林里时，野兽的守候似乎结束了。当他听见商人说起自己心地善良的女儿时，野兽心中开始燃起希望。接着，好心的精灵开始展开她的计划……

31

A WEDDING AT THE GREAT HALL

"Beauty," the fairy said, "your willingness to sacrifice your own life to save your father's proved that you were truly capable of the kind of love and *devotion* that was needed to free the prince."

"Beauty," said the prince, "you — only you — accepted me because you saw that underneath my physical appearance, I had a generous, gentle heart that would love and protect you always."

After the tale was told, they were all magically transported into the castle. As they walked down the great hall, they passed the gilded mirror. Beauty peered into it. This time, she saw only the reflection cast by a couple happily walking arm in arm toward their wedding. There were no mysterious visions of the past or unwelcome images.

To Beauty's surprise, her whole family was in the great

三十一

大厅里的婚礼

"贝蒂，"精灵说，"你愿意牺牲自己来换取父亲的性命，证明你有爱心和奉献精神，这正是解救王子所需要的。"

"贝蒂，"王子说，"你——也只有你——才会接受我，因为你看见我外表下隐藏着一颗慷慨、温柔的心，它会一直爱着你、保护你。"

故事讲完后，他们又神奇地转到了城堡里。他们走过大厅时，经过镀金的镜子，贝蒂朝里面瞥了一眼，这一次，她只看见一对新人快乐地手挽手走向婚礼现场，再也看不见过去神秘的、讨厌的影像。

让贝蒂吃惊的是，她的家人此刻都在大厅里。是仁慈的

hall. They had been brought there by the good fairy's magic to celebrate the happy event.

"True happiness is your reward, Beauty," the fairy said, "for being wise and choosing virtue over good looks and wit. You have found a person in whom all those qualities *exist*. I know becoming queen will never change your true heart."

Beauty's father was overwhelmed with happiness for his daughter. Her brothers were thrilled by her good fortune. Only Elise and Rene sneered at her from a corner of the great hall. They were furious at how Beauty's situation with the Beast had turned out.

"Ladies," the fairy said, "your hearts are filled with anger and jealousy. To match your hearts of stone, you shall both become statues guarding the doors of your sister's palace. But beneath the stone you will keep your sense of reason so that you can always reflect on the faults that led to your transformation. Perhaps in time you will *repent*."

Elise and Rene could not answer the fairy, for they were frozen by fear.

"Wait, dear fairy," Beauty called out. "Please do not harm my sisters. In time, I am sure they will change," she said lovingly, not wanting them to suffer the kind of fate her beloved Beast had endured.

精灵用魔法把他们带来庆祝这快乐的聚会。

"贝蒂，获得真正的幸福是对你的奖赏。"精灵说，"因为你如此明智，选择了美德而不是外表和智力。你现在找到了一个品德优良、长相英俊又富有才智的人。你现在成了王后，但是我相信你的真心永远不会改变。"

贝蒂的父亲为女儿感到无比喜悦，她的两个哥哥也为她的好运激动不已，只有伊莉斯和雷内站在大厅的角落里对她冷嘲热讽。她们俩对贝蒂和野兽现在的结局大为恼火。

"女士们，"精灵说，"你们内心充满了愤怒和嫉妒。为了与你们的铁石心肠相称，你们俩将变成雕像守卫在妹妹的宫殿门口。可是，在雕像的外表下，你们仍然保持清醒，这样就能一直反省你们犯下的过错，或许最后你们能够悔悟。"

伊莉斯和雷内哑口无言，她们早已吓呆了。

"等等，亲爱的精灵，"贝蒂大叫起来，"请别伤害我姐姐，我敢保证她们会改过来的。"她深情地说，不想让姐姐遭受她深爱着的野兽那种命运。

"Most human faults can be changed in time," the fairy answered her. "But the faults of your sisters — hatred and envy — are almost impossible to alter. Still, I will grant your wish. Maybe your goodness will rub off on them after all. Stranger things have happened."

Beauty couldn't agree more. Surely, stranger things had happened!

With a stroke of her wand, the fairy transformed the hall into a wedding banquet. Beauty and her beloved prince were married, to the great joy of their families and their subjects. Afterward, they returned to the official palace.

But Beauty and the prince loved the enchantments at the summer palace, and they wanted to live there.

"Now that the spell is broken," the kind fairy said, "you both must accept your *responsibilities*. But you can visit the summer palace whenever you wish. I will always ensure that the magic there endures to delight you both."

And it did.

"人类大多数缺点都能及时得到改正，"精灵回答她，"可是你姐姐身上的缺点——仇恨和嫉妒——几乎不可能纠正过来。不过，我还是答应你的请求，或许你的好心肠能够消除它们。毕竟，比这更奇特的事情都发生了。"

贝蒂非常同意。当然，更奇特的事情的确已经发生了！

精灵用她的魔杖让整个大厅变成了一场婚宴。贝蒂和她深爱的王子结婚了，这让他们的家人和王子的随从狂喜不已。婚宴之后，他们回到正宫。

可是贝蒂和王子喜欢这个充满魅力的夏宫，他们想要住在那里。

"既然符咒已经解除，"和善的精灵说，"你们两人必须担当起自己的职责。不过只要你们喜欢，可以随时拜访夏宫。我会一直保留这里的魔法，让你们高兴。"

后来的一切正如精灵所言。

EPILOGUE

Beauty and the prince were grateful for the good fairy's favors. Whenever they wanted to return to the summer palace, they only had to summon the unicorn that led the golden chariot, an enchanted wedding gift from the kind fairy. It would appear in a flash and transport them to the castle in the blink of an eye.

Beauty and the prince visited the palace often to enjoy the gazebo, the theater room and all of the other splendors there. They spent most of their time enjoying the rose garden and its lovely flowers, which were a symbol of their deep love and eternal happiness.

Although they were mortal, their time on earth seemed to be an endless enchantment that enabled them to truly live happily every after.

尾　声

　　贝蒂和王子感激仁慈的精灵对他们的恩惠。每当他们想回夏宫的时候，只需召唤拉着金色战车的独角兽就行了，这是精灵送给他们的魔幻般的新婚礼物。独角兽听到召唤后瞬间就会出现，而且一眨眼就把他们送到城堡。

　　贝蒂和王子常回到宫殿里重游观景台、剧场，还有其他充满奇迹的地方。不过，他们把大部分时间都花在玫瑰园里，欣赏着可爱的花儿，那里象征着他们深厚的爱情和永恒的幸福。

　　尽管他们是凡人，可是，他们在尘世的光阴就像充满了永不休止的魔力，使得他们从此能够过上真正快乐的生活。

词 汇 表

1

elegant ['eligənt] *adj.* 高雅的；高尚的；优美的
handsome ['hænsəm] *adj.* 漂亮的，英俊的
disposition [,dispə'ziʃən] *n.* 性情；脾气

2

dishonest [dis'ɔnist] *adj.* 欺诈的；不诚实的
livestock ['laivstɔk] *n.* 家畜
laundry ['lɔ:ndri] *n.* 洗衣店

5

activity [æk'tiviti] *n.* 活跃；景气
merchandise ['mə:tʃəndaiz] *n.* 商品；货物

8

magnificent [mæg'nifisnt] *adj.* 关壮观的；雄伟的
arbor ['a:bɔ:] *n.* 亭子；凉亭
labyrinth ['læbərinθ] *n.* 迷宫

12

imprisonment [im'priznmənt] *n.* 关押；监禁
onion ['ʌnjən] *n.* 洋葱

15

splendor ['splendər] *n.* 壮观；光辉；光彩
library ['laibrəri] *n.* 图书馆；书房
harp [ha:p] *n.* 竖琴
amusement [ə'mju:zmənt] *n.* 娱乐；乐趣；消遣
unfold [ʌn'fəuld] *v.* 展开；显露；表明

17

precious ['preʃəs] *adj.* 宝贵的；高价的
ferocious [fə'rəuʃəs] *adj.* 凶猛的；残暴的
ugly ['ʌgli] *adj.* 难看的；丑陋的

19

parrot ['pærət] *n.* 鹦鹉；应声虫
sparrow ['spærəu] *n.* 麻雀
curiosity [,kjuəri'ɔsiti] *n.* 好奇；求知欲
sincerely [sin'siəli] *adv.* 诚恳地；真挚地

22

theater ['θiətə] *n.* 剧院；剧场
candelabra [,kændi'la:brə] *n.* 枝状大烛台
impulsively [im'pʌlsivli] *adv.* 有推动力地
murmur ['mə:mə] *v.* 低声说；嘟囔

24

reunion ['ri:'ju:njən] *n.* 团圆
princess ['prinses] *adj.* 公主；王妃；公爵夫人
mean [mi:n] *adj.* 卑贱的

26

pond [pɔnd] *n.* 池塘
sadly ['sædli] *adv.* 悲痛地；伤心地

27

melody ['melədi] *n.* 美的音乐；美的曲调
melancholy ['melənkəli] *n.* 悲伤；忧郁
wilt [wilt] *v.* 枯萎；失去力气
pulse [pʌls] *n.* 脉搏；情绪
cannon ['kænən] *n.* 大炮

29

transformation [ˌtrænsfə'meiʃən] *n.* 转变；改变
alliance [ə'laiəns] *n.* 同盟；联盟
imp [imp] *n.* 小鬼；小魔鬼

30

retreat [ri'triːt] *n.* 避难所
hesitation [ˌhezi'teiʃən] *n.* 踌躇；迟疑
insignificant [ˌinsig'nifikənt] *adj.* 无关重要的；小的
insolence ['insələns] *n.* 傲慢；蛮横
hideous ['hidiəs] *adj.* 丑恶的；可憎的；讨厌的

31

devotion [di'vənʃən] *n.* 献身；热爱
exist [ig'zist] *v.* 有；存在；生存
repent [ri'pent] *v.* 悔恨；后悔
responsibility [risˌpɔnsə'biliti] *n.* 责任；负担

Beauty and the Beast